Life Application Bible Studies
1, 2 & 3 JOHN

APPLICATION® BIBLE STUDIES

Part 1:
Complete text of 1, 2 & 3 John with study notes and features from the *Life Application Study Bible*

Part 2:
Thirteen lessons for individual or group study

Study questions written and edited by

Linda Chaffee Taylor
Rev. David R. Veerman
Dr. James C. Galvin
Dr. Bruce B. Barton
Daryl J. Lucas

New Living Translation®

Tyndale House Publishers, Inc.
Carol Stream, Illinois

1, 2 & 3 john

Visit Tyndale online at www.newlivingtranslation.com and www.tyndale.com.

New Living Translation, NLT, the New Living Translation logo, *Life Application*, *Life App*, and the Life App logo are registered trademarks of Tyndale House Publishers, Inc.

Life Application Bible Studies: 1, 2 & 3 John

Copyright © 1999, 2010 by Tyndale House Publishers, Inc., Carol Stream, Illinois 60188. All rights reserved.

Life Application notes and features copyright © 1988, 1989, 1990, 1991, 1993, 1996, 2004 by Tyndale House Publishers, Inc., Carol Stream, Illinois 60188. All rights reserved.

Cover photograph copyright © by Vernon Wiley/Getty Images. All rights reserved.

The text of 1, 2 & 3 John is from the *Holy Bible,* New Living Translation, copyright © 1996, 2004, 2007 by Tyndale House Foundation. All rights reserved.

For information about special discounts for bulk purchases, please contact Tyndale House Publishers at csresponse@tyndale.com, or call 1-800-323-9400.

ISBN 978-1-4143-2654-2

Printed in the United States of America

23   22   21   20   19   18   17
9   8   7   6   5   4   3

CONTENTS

A NOTE TO READERS

The *Holy Bible*, New Living Translation, was first published in 1996. It quickly became one of the most popular Bible translations in the English-speaking world. While the NLT's influence was rapidly growing, the Bible Translation Committee determined that an additional investment in scholarly review and text refinement could make it even better. So shortly after its initial publication, the committee began an eight-year process with the purpose of increasing the level of the NLT's precision without sacrificing its easy-to-understand quality. This second-generation text was completed in 2004 and is reflected in this edition of the New Living Translation. An additional update with minor changes was subsequently introduced in 2007.

The goal of any Bible translation is to convey the meaning and content of the ancient Hebrew, Aramaic, and Greek texts as accurately as possible to contemporary readers. The challenge for our translators was to create a text that would communicate as clearly and powerfully to today's readers as the original texts did to readers and listeners in the ancient biblical world. The resulting translation is easy to read and understand, while also accurately communicating the meaning and content of the original biblical texts. The NLT is a general-purpose text especially good for study, devotional reading, and reading aloud in worship services.

We believe that the New Living Translation—which combines the latest biblical scholarship with a clear, dynamic writing style—will communicate God's word powerfully to all who read it. We publish it with the prayer that God will use it to speak his timeless truth to the church and the world in a fresh, new way.

The Publishers
October 2007

INTRODUCTION TO THE
NEW LIVING TRANSLATION

Translation Philosophy and Methodology

English Bible translations tend to be governed by one of two general translation theories. The first theory has been called "formal-equivalence," "literal," or "word-for-word" translation. According to this theory, the translator attempts to render each word of the original language into English and seeks to preserve the original syntax and sentence structure as much as possible in translation. The second theory has been called "dynamic-equivalence," "functional-equivalence," or "thought-for-thought" translation. The goal of this translation theory is to produce in English the closest natural equivalent of the message expressed by the original-language text, both in meaning and in style.

Both of these translation theories have their strengths. A formal-equivalence translation preserves aspects of the original text—including ancient idioms, term consistency, and original-language syntax—that are valuable for scholars and professional study. It allows a reader to trace formal elements of the original-language text through the English translation. A dynamic-equivalence translation, on the other hand, focuses on translating the message of the original-language text. It ensures that the meaning of the text is readily apparent to the contemporary reader. This allows the message to come through with immediacy, without requiring the reader to struggle with foreign idioms and awkward syntax. It also facilitates serious study of the text's message and clarity in both devotional and public reading.

The pure application of either of these translation philosophies would create translations at opposite ends of the translation spectrum. But in reality, all translations contain a mixture of these two philosophies. A purely formal-equivalence translation would be unintelligible in English, and a purely dynamic-equivalence translation would risk being unfaithful to the original. That is why translations shaped by dynamic-equivalence theory are usually quite literal when the original text is relatively clear, and the translations shaped by formal-equivalence theory are sometimes quite dynamic when the original text is obscure.

The translators of the New Living Translation set out to render the message of the original texts of Scripture into clear, contemporary English. As they did so, they kept the concerns of both formal-equivalence and dynamic-equivalence in mind. On the one hand, they translated as simply and literally as possible when that approach yielded an accurate, clear, and natural English text. Many words and phrases were rendered literally and consistently into English, preserving essential literary and rhetorical devices, ancient metaphors, and word choices that give structure to the text and provide echoes of meaning from one passage to the next.

On the other hand, the translators rendered the message more dynamically when the literal rendering was hard to understand, was misleading, or yielded archaic or foreign wording. They clarified difficult metaphors and terms to aid in the reader's understanding. The translators first struggled with the meaning of the words and phrases in the ancient context; then they rendered the message into clear, natural English. Their goal was to be both faithful to the ancient texts and eminently readable. The result is a translation that is both exegetically accurate and idiomatically powerful.

Translation Process and Team

To produce an accurate translation of the Bible into contemporary English, the translation team needed the skills necessary to enter into the thought patterns of the ancient authors and then to render their ideas, connotations, and effects into clear, contemporary English.

To begin this process, qualified biblical scholars were needed to interpret the meaning of the original text and to check it against our base English translation. In order to guard against personal and theological biases, the scholars needed to represent a diverse group of evangelicals who would employ the best exegetical tools. Then to work alongside the scholars, skilled English stylists were needed to shape the text into clear, contemporary English.

With these concerns in mind, the Bible Translation Committee recruited teams of scholars that represented a broad spectrum of denominations, theological perspectives, and backgrounds within the worldwide evangelical community. Each book of the Bible was assigned to three different scholars with proven expertise in the book or group of books to be reviewed. Each of these scholars made a thorough review of a base translation and submitted suggested revisions to the appropriate Senior Translator. The Senior Translator then reviewed and summarized these suggestions and proposed a first-draft revision of the base text. This draft served as the basis for several additional phases of exegetical and stylistic committee review. Then the Bible Translation Committee jointly reviewed and approved every verse of the final translation.

Throughout the translation and editing process, the Senior Translators and their scholar teams were given a chance to review the editing done by the team of stylists. This ensured that exegetical errors would not be introduced late in the process and that the entire Bible Translation Committee was happy with the final result. By choosing a team of qualified scholars and skilled stylists and by setting up a process that allowed their interaction throughout the process, the New Living Translation has been refined to preserve the essential formal elements of the original biblical texts, while also creating a clear, understandable English text.

The New Living Translation was first published in 1996. Shortly after its initial publication, the Bible Translation Committee began a process of further committee review and translation refinement. The purpose of this continued revision was to increase the level of precision without sacrificing the text's easy-to-understand quality. This second-edition text was completed in 2004, and an additional update with minor changes was subsequently introduced in 2007. This printing of the New Living Translation reflects the updated 2007 text.

Written to Be Read Aloud
It is evident in Scripture that the biblical documents were written to be read aloud, often in public worship (see Nehemiah 8; Luke 4:16-20; 1 Timothy 4:13; Revelation 1:3). It is still the case today that more people will hear the Bible read aloud in church than are likely to read it for themselves. Therefore, a new translation must communicate with clarity and power when it is read publicly. Clarity was a primary goal for the NLT translators, not only to facilitate private reading and understanding, but also to ensure that it would be excellent for public reading and make an immediate and powerful impact on any listener.

The Texts behind the New Living Translation
The Old Testament translators used the Masoretic Text of the Hebrew Bible as represented in *Biblia Hebraica Stuttgartensia* (1977), with its extensive system of textual notes; this is an update of Rudolf Kittel's *Biblia Hebraica* (Stuttgart, 1937). The translators also further compared the Dead Sea Scrolls, the Septuagint and other Greek manuscripts, the Samaritan Pentateuch, the Syriac Peshitta, the Latin Vulgate, and any other versions or manuscripts that shed light on the meaning of difficult passages.

The New Testament translators used the two standard editions of the Greek New Testament: the *Greek New Testament,* published by the United Bible Societies (UBS, fourth revised edition, 1993), and *Novum Testamentum Graece,* edited by Nestle and Aland (NA, twenty-seventh edition, 1993). These two editions, which have the same text but differ in punctuation and textual notes, represent, for the most part, the best in modern textual scholarship. However, in cases where strong textual or other scholarly evidence supported the decision, the translators sometimes chose to differ from the UBS and NA Greek texts and followed variant readings found in other ancient witnesses. Significant textual variants of this sort are always noted in the textual notes of the New Living Translation.

Translation Issues
The translators have made a conscious effort to provide a text that can be easily understood by the typical reader of modern English. To this end, we sought to use only vocabulary and

language structures in common use today. We avoided using language likely to become quickly dated or that reflects only a narrow subdialect of English, with the goal of making the New Living Translation as broadly useful and timeless as possible.

But our concern for readability goes beyond the concerns of vocabulary and sentence structure. We are also concerned about historical and cultural barriers to understanding the Bible, and we have sought to translate terms shrouded in history and culture in ways that can be immediately understood. To this end:

- We have converted ancient weights and measures (for example, "ephah" [a unit of dry volume] or "cubit" [a unit of length]) to modern English (American) equivalents, since the ancient measures are not generally meaningful to today's readers. Then in the textual footnotes we offer the literal Hebrew, Aramaic, or Greek measures, along with modern metric equivalents.
- Instead of translating ancient currency values literally, we have expressed them in common terms that communicate the message. For example, in the Old Testament, "ten shekels of silver" becomes "ten pieces of silver" to convey the intended message. In the New Testament, we have often translated the "denarius" as "the normal daily wage" to facilitate understanding. Then a footnote offers: "Greek *a denarius,* the payment for a full day's labor." In general, we give a clear English rendering and then state the literal Hebrew, Aramaic, or Greek in a textual footnote.
- Since the names of Hebrew months are unknown to most contemporary readers, and since the Hebrew lunar calendar fluctuates from year to year in relation to the solar calendar used today, we have looked for clear ways to communicate the time of year the Hebrew months (such as Abib) refer to. When an expanded or interpretive rendering is given in the text, a textual note gives the literal rendering. Where it is possible to define a specific ancient date in terms of our modern calendar, we use modern dates in the text. A textual footnote then gives the literal Hebrew date and states the rationale for our rendering. For example, Ezra 6:15 pinpoints the date when the postexilic Temple was completed in Jerusalem: "the third day of the month Adar." This was during the sixth year of King Darius's reign (that is, 515 B.C.). We have translated that date as March 12, with a footnote giving the Hebrew and identifying the year as 515 B.C.
- Since ancient references to the time of day differ from our modern methods of denoting time, we have used renderings that are instantly understandable to the modern reader. Accordingly, we have rendered specific times of day by using approximate equivalents in terms of our common "o'clock" system. On occasion, translations such as "at dawn the next morning" or "as the sun was setting" have been used when the biblical reference is more general.
- When the meaning of a proper name (or a wordplay inherent in a proper name) is relevant to the message of the text, its meaning is often illuminated with a textual footnote. For example, in Exodus 2:10 the text reads: "The princess named him Moses, for she explained, 'I lifted him out of the water.' " The accompanying footnote reads: "*Moses* sounds like a Hebrew term that means 'to lift out.' "

  Sometimes, when the actual meaning of a name is clear, that meaning is included in parentheses within the text itself. For example, the text at Genesis 16:11 reads: "You are to name him Ishmael *(which means 'God hears'),* for the LORD has heard your cry of distress." Since the original hearers and readers would have instantly understood the meaning of the name "Ishmael," we have provided modern readers with the same information so they can experience the text in a similar way.
- Many words and phrases carry a great deal of cultural meaning that was obvious to the original readers but needs explanation in our own culture. For example, the phrase "they beat their breasts" (Luke 23:48) in ancient times meant that people were very upset, often in mourning. In our translation we chose to translate this phrase dynamically for clarity: "They went home *in deep sorrow.*" Then we included a footnote with the literal Greek, which reads: "Greek *went home beating their breasts.*" In other similar cases, however, we have sometimes chosen to illuminate the existing literal expression to make it immediately understandable. For example, here we might have expanded the literal Greek phrase to read: "They went home

beating their breasts *in sorrow.*" If we had done this, we would not have included a textual footnote, since the literal Greek clearly appears in translation.

- Metaphorical language is sometimes difficult for contemporary readers to understand, so at times we have chosen to translate or illuminate the meaning of a metaphor. For example, the ancient poet writes, "Your neck is *like* the tower of David" (Song of Songs 4:4). We have rendered it "Your neck is *as beautiful as* the tower of David" to clarify the intended positive meaning of the simile. Another example comes in Ecclesiastes 12:3, which can be literally rendered: "Remember him . . . when the grinding women cease because they are few, and the women who look through the windows see dimly." We have rendered it: "Remember him before your teeth—your few remaining servants—stop grinding; and before your eyes—the women looking through the windows—see dimly." We clarified such metaphors only when we believed a typical reader might be confused by the literal text.

- When the content of the original language text is poetic in character, we have rendered it in English poetic form. We sought to break lines in ways that clarify and highlight the relationships between phrases of the text. Hebrew poetry often uses parallelism, a literary form where a second phrase (or in some instances a third or fourth) echoes the initial phrase in some way. In Hebrew parallelism, the subsequent parallel phrases continue, while also furthering and sharpening, the thought expressed in the initial line or phrase. Whenever possible, we sought to represent these parallel phrases in natural poetic English.

- The Greek term *hoi Ioudaioi* is literally translated "the Jews" in many English translations. In the Gospel of John, however, this term doesn't always refer to the Jewish people generally. In some contexts, it refers more particularly to the Jewish religious leaders. We have attempted to capture the meaning in these different contexts by using terms such as "the people" (with a footnote: Greek *the Jewish people*) or "the Jewish leaders," where appropriate.

- One challenge we faced was how to translate accurately the ancient biblical text that was originally written in a context where male-oriented terms were used to refer to humanity generally. We needed to respect the nature of the ancient context while also trying to make the translation clear to a modern audience that tends to read male-oriented language as applying only to males. Often the original text, though using masculine nouns and pronouns, clearly intends that the message be applied to both men and women. A typical example is found in the New Testament letters, where the believers are called "brothers" (*adelphoi*). Yet it is clear from the content of these letters that they were addressed to all the believers—male and female. Thus, we have usually translated this Greek word as "brothers and sisters" in order to represent the historical situation more accurately.

We have also been sensitive to passages where the text applies generally to human beings or to the human condition. In some instances we have used plural pronouns (they, them) in place of the masculine singular (he, him). For example, a traditional rendering of Proverbs 22:6 is: "Train up a child in the way he should go, and when he is old he will not turn from it." We have rendered it: "Direct your children onto the right path, and when they are older, they will not leave it." At times, we have also replaced third person pronouns with the second person to ensure clarity. A traditional rendering of Proverbs 26:27 is: "He who digs a pit will fall into it, and he who rolls a stone, it will come back on him." We have rendered it: "If you set a trap for others, you will get caught in it yourself. If you roll a boulder down on others, it will crush you instead."

We should emphasize, however, that all masculine nouns and pronouns used to represent God (for example, "Father") have been maintained without exception. All decisions of this kind have been driven by the concern to reflect accurately the intended meaning of the original texts of Scripture.

Lexical Consistency in Terminology
For the sake of clarity, we have translated certain original-language terms consistently, especially within synoptic passages and for commonly repeated rhetorical phrases, and within

certain word categories such as divine names and non-theological technical terminology (e.g., liturgical, legal, cultural, zoological, and botanical terms). For theological terms, we have allowed a greater semantic range of acceptable English words or phrases for a single Hebrew or Greek word. We have avoided some theological terms that are not readily understood by many modern readers. For example, we avoided using words such as "justification" and "sanctification," which are carryovers from Latin translations. In place of these words, we have provided renderings such as "made right with God" and "made holy."

The Spelling of Proper Names

Many individuals in the Bible, especially the Old Testament, are known by more than one name (e.g., Uzziah/Azariah). For the sake of clarity, we have tried to use a single spelling for any one individual, footnoting the literal spelling whenever we differ from it. This is especially helpful in delineating the kings of Israel and Judah. King Joash/Jehoash of Israel has been consistently called Jehoash, while King Joash/Jehoash of Judah is called Joash. A similar distinction has been used to distinguish between Joram/Jehoram of Israel and Joram/Jehoram of Judah. All such decisions were made with the goal of clarifying the text for the reader. When the ancient biblical writers clearly had a theological purpose in their choice of a variant name (e.g., Esh-baal/Ishbosheth), the different names have been maintained with an explanatory footnote.

For the names Jacob and Israel, which are used interchangeably for both the individual patriarch and the nation, we generally render it "Israel" when it refers to the nation and "Jacob" when it refers to the individual. When our rendering of the name differs from the underlying Hebrew text, we provide a textual footnote, which includes this explanation: "The names 'Jacob' and 'Israel' are often interchanged throughout the Old Testament, referring sometimes to the individual patriarch and sometimes to the nation."

The Rendering of Divine Names

All appearances of *'el, 'elohim,* or *'eloah* have been translated "God," except where the context demands the translation "god(s)." We have generally rendered the tetragrammaton (*YHWH*) consistently as "the LORD," utilizing a form with small capitals that is common among English translations. This will distinguish it from the name *'adonai,* which we render "Lord." When *'adonai* and *YHWH* appear together, we have rendered it "Sovereign LORD." This also distinguishes *'adonai YHWH* from cases where *YHWH* appears with *'elohim,* which is rendered "LORD God." When *YH* (the short form of *YHWH*) and *YHWH* appear together, we have rendered it "LORD GOD." When *YHWH* appears with the term *tseba'oth,* we have rendered it "LORD of Heaven's Armies" to translate the meaning of the name. In a few cases, we have utilized the transliteration, *Yahweh,* when the personal character of the name is being invoked in contrast to another divine name or the name of some other god (for example, see Exodus 3:15; 6:2-3).

In the Gospels and Acts, the Greek word *christos* has been translated as "Messiah" when the context assumes a Jewish audience. When a Gentile audience can be assumed (which is consistently the case in the Epistles and Revelation), *christos* has been translated as "Christ." The Greek word *kurios* is consistently translated "Lord," except that it is translated "LORD" wherever the New Testament text explicitly quotes from the Old Testament, and the text there has it in small capitals.

Textual Footnotes

The New Living Translation provides several kinds of textual footnotes, all designated in the text with an asterisk:

- When for the sake of clarity the NLT renders a difficult or potentially confusing phrase dynamically, we generally give the literal rendering in a textual footnote. This allows the reader to see the literal source of our dynamic rendering and how our translation relates to other more literal translations. These notes are prefaced with "Hebrew," "Aramaic," or "Greek," identifying the language of the underlying source text. For example, in Acts 2:42 we translated the literal "breaking of bread" (from the Greek) as "the Lord's Supper" to clarify that this verse refers to the ceremonial practice of the church rather than just an ordinary meal. Then we attached a footnote to "the Lord's Supper," which reads: "Greek *the breaking of bread.*"

- Textual footnotes are also used to show alternative renderings, prefaced with the word "Or." These normally occur for passages where an aspect of the meaning is debated. On occasion, we also provide notes on words or phrases that represent a departure from long-standing tradition. These notes are prefaced with "Tradition-ally rendered." For example, the footnote to the translation "serious skin disease" at Leviticus 13:2 says: "Traditionally rendered *leprosy.* The Hebrew word used throughout this passage is used to describe various skin diseases."

- When our translators follow a textual variant that differs significantly from our stan-dard Hebrew or Greek texts (listed earlier), we document that difference with a foot-note. We also footnote cases when the NLT excludes a passage that is included in the Greek text known as the *Textus Receptus* (and familiar to readers through its transla-tion in the King James Version). In such cases, we offer a translation of the excluded text in a footnote, even though it is generally recognized as a later addition to the Greek text and not part of the original Greek New Testament.

- All Old Testament passages that are quoted in the New Testament are identified by a textual footnote at the New Testament location. When the New Testament clearly quotes from the Greek translation of the Old Testament, and when it differs signifi-cantly in wording from the Hebrew text, we also place a textual footnote at the Old Testament location. This note includes a rendering of the Greek version, along with a cross-reference to the New Testament passage(s) where it is cited (for example, see notes on Psalms 8:2; 53:3; Proverbs 3:12).

- Some textual footnotes provide cultural and historical information on places, things, and people in the Bible that are probably obscure to modern readers. Such notes should aid the reader in understanding the message of the text. For example, in Acts 12:1, "King Herod" is named in this translation as "King Herod Agrippa" and is iden-tified in a footnote as being "the nephew of Herod Antipas and a grandson of Herod the Great."

- When the meaning of a proper name (or a wordplay inherent in a proper name) is relevant to the meaning of the text, it is either illuminated with a textual footnote or included within parentheses in the text itself. For example, the footnote concerning the name "Eve" at Genesis 3:20 reads: "*Eve* sounds like a Hebrew term that means 'to give life.' " This wordplay in the Hebrew illuminates the meaning of the text, which goes on to say that Eve "would be the mother of all who live."

AS WE SUBMIT this translation for publication, we recognize that any translation of the Scrip-tures is subject to limitations and imperfections. Anyone who has attempted to communi-cate the richness of God's Word into another language will realize it is impossible to make a perfect translation. Recognizing these limitations, we sought God's guidance and wisdom throughout this project. Now we pray that he will accept our efforts and use this translation for the benefit of the church and of all people.

We pray that the New Living Translation will overcome some of the barriers of history, cul-ture, and language that have kept people from reading and understanding God's Word. We hope that readers unfamiliar with the Bible will find the words clear and easy to understand and that readers well versed in the Scriptures will gain a fresh perspective. We pray that readers will gain insight and wisdom for living, but most of all that they will meet the God of the Bible and be forever changed by knowing him.

The Bible Translation Committee
October 2007

WHY THE
LIFE APPLICATION STUDY BIBLE
IS UNIQUE

Have you ever opened your Bible and asked the following:

- What does this passage really mean?
- How does it apply to my life?
- Why does some of the Bible seem irrelevant?
- What do these ancient cultures have to do with today?
- I love God; why can't I understand what he is saying to me through his word?
- What's going on in the lives of these Bible people?

Many Christians do not read the Bible regularly. Why? Because in the pressures of daily living they cannot find a connection between the timeless principles of Scripture and the ever-present problems of day-by-day living.

God urges us to apply his word (Isaiah 42:23; 1 Corinthians 10:11; 2 Thessalonians 3:4), but too often we stop at accumulating Bible knowledge. This is why the *Life Application Study Bible* was developed—to show how to put into practice what we have learned.

Applying God's word is a vital part of one's relationship with God; it is the evidence that we are obeying him. The difficulty in applying the Bible is not with the Bible itself, but with the reader's inability to bridge the gap between the past and present, the conceptual and practical. When we don't or can't do this, spiritual dryness, shallowness, and indifference are the results.

The words of Scripture itself cry out to us, "But don't just listen to God's word. You must do what it says. Otherwise, you are only fooling yourselves" (James 1:22). The *Life Application Study Bible* helps us to obey God's word. Developed by an interdenominational team of pastors, scholars, family counselors, and a national organization dedicated to promoting God's word and spreading the gospel, the *Life Application Study Bible* took many years to complete. All the work was reviewed by several renowned theologians under the directorship of Dr. Kenneth Kantzer.

The *Life Application Study Bible* does what a good resource Bible should: It helps you understand the context of a passage, gives important background and historical information, explains difficult words and phrases, and helps you see the interrelationship of Scripture. But it does much more. The *Life Application Study Bible* goes deeper into God's word, helping you discover the timeless truth being communicated, see the relevance for your life, and make a personal application. While some study Bibles attempt application, over 75 percent of this Bible is application oriented. The notes answer the questions "So what?" and "What does this passage mean to me, my family, my friends, my job, my neighborhood, my church, my country?"

Imagine reading a familiar passage of Scripture and gaining fresh insight, as if it were the first time you had ever read it. How much richer your life would be if you left each Bible reading with a new perspective and a small change for the better. A small change every day adds up to a changed life—and that is the very purpose of Scripture.

WHAT IS APPLICATION?

The best way to define application is to first determine what it is *not*. Application is *not* just accumulating knowledge. Accumulating knowledge helps us discover and understand facts and concepts, but it stops there. History is filled with philosophers who knew what the Bible said but failed to apply it to their lives, keeping them from believing and changing. Many think that understanding is the end goal of Bible study, but it is really only the beginning.

Application is *not* just illustration. Illustration only tells us how someone else handled a similar situation. While we may empathize with that person, we still have little direction for our personal situation.

Application is *not* just making a passage "relevant." Making the Bible relevant only helps us to see that the same lessons that were true in Bible times are true today; it does not show us how to apply them to the problems and pressures of our individual lives.

What, then, is application? Application begins by knowing and understanding God's word and its timeless truths. *But you cannot stop there.* If you do, God's word may not change your life, and it may become dull, difficult, tedious, and tiring. A good application focuses the truth of God's word, shows the reader what to do about what is being read, and motivates the reader to respond to what God is teaching. All three are essential to application.

Application is putting into practice what we already know (see Mark 4:24 and Hebrews 5:14) and answering the question "So what?" by confronting us with the right questions and motivating us to take action (see 1 John 2:5-6 and James 2:26). Application is deeply personal—unique for each individual. It makes a relevant truth a personal truth and involves developing a strategy and action plan to live your life in harmony with the Bible. It is the biblical "how to" of life.

You may ask, "How can your application notes be relevant to my life?" Each application note has three parts: (1) an *explanation*, which ties the note directly to the Scripture passage and sets up the truth that is being taught; (2) the *bridge*, which explains the timeless truth and makes it relevant for today; (3) the *application*, which shows you how to take the timeless truth and apply it to your personal situation. No note, by itself, can apply Scripture directly to your life. It can only teach, direct, lead, guide, inspire, recommend, and urge. It can give you the resources and direction you need to apply the Bible, but only you can take these resources and put them into practice.

A good note, therefore, should not only give you knowledge and understanding but point you to application. Before you buy any kind of resource study Bible, you should evaluate the notes and ask the following questions: (1) Does the note contain enough information to help me understand the point of the Scripture passage? (2) Does the note assume I know more than I do? (3) Does the note avoid denominational bias? (4) Do the notes touch most of life's experiences? (5) Does the note help me apply God's word?

FEATURES OF THE
LIFE APPLICATION STUDY BIBLE

NOTES
In addition to providing the reader with many application notes, the *Life Application Study Bible* also offers several kinds of explanatory notes, which help the reader understand culture, history, context, difficult-to-understand passages, background, places, theological concepts, and the relationship of various passages in Scripture to other passages.

BOOK INTRODUCTIONS
Each book introduction is divided into several easy-to-find parts:

Timeline. A guide that puts the Bible book into its historical setting. It lists the key events and the dates when they occurred.

Vital Statistics. A list of straight facts about the book—those pieces of information you need to know at a glance.

Overview. A summary of the book with general lessons and applications that can be learned from the book as a whole.

Blueprint. The outline of the book. It is printed in easy-to-understand language and is designed for easy memorization. To the right of each main heading is a key lesson that is taught in that particular section.

Megathemes. A section that gives the main themes of the Bible book, explains their significance, and then tells you why they are still important for us today.

Map. If included, this shows the key places found in that book and retells the story of the book from a geographical point of view.

OUTLINE
The *Life Application Study Bible* has a new, custom-made outline that was designed specifically from an application point of view. Several unique features should be noted:

1. To avoid confusion and to aid memory work, the book outline has only three levels for headings. Main outline heads are marked with a capital letter. Subheads are marked by a number. Minor explanatory heads have no letter or number.

2. Each main outline head marked by a letter also has a brief paragraph below it summarizing the Bible text and offering a general application.

3. Parallel passages are listed where they apply.

PERSONALITY PROFILES
Among the unique features of this Bible are the profiles of key Bible people, including their strengths and weaknesses, greatest accomplishments and mistakes, and key lessons from their lives.

MAPS
The *Life Application Study Bible* has a thorough and comprehensive Bible atlas built right into the book. There are two kinds of maps: a book-introduction map, telling the story of the book, and thumbnail maps in the notes, plotting most geographic movements.

CHARTS AND DIAGRAMS
Many charts and diagrams are included to help the reader better visualize difficult concepts or relationships. Most charts not only present the needed information but show the significance of the information as well.

CROSS-REFERENCES
An updated, exhaustive cross-reference system in the margins of the Bible text helps the reader find related passages quickly.

TEXTUAL NOTES
Directly related to the text of the New Living Translation, the textual notes provide explanations on certain wording in the translation, alternate translations, and information about readings in the ancient manuscripts.

HIGHLIGHTED NOTES
In each Bible study lesson, you will be asked to read specific notes as part of your preparation. These notes have each been highlighted by a bullet (•) so that you can find them easily.

1, 2 & 3 JOHN

1 JOHN

"A GOOD man . . . yes . . . perhaps one of the best who ever lived . . . but just a man," say many. Others disagree, claiming that he suffered from delusions of grandeur—a "messiah complex." And the argument rages over the true identity of this man called Jesus. Suggestions have ranged from "simple teacher" to "egomaniac" and "misguided fool." Whoever he was, all would agree that Jesus left his mark on history.

Hearing these discussions, even Christians can begin to wonder and doubt. Is Jesus really God? Did he come to save sinners like us? Does God care about me?

First John was written to dispel doubts and to build assurance by presenting a clear picture of Christ. Entering history, Jesus was and is God in the flesh and God in focus—seen, heard, and touched by the author of this letter, John the apostle. John walked and talked with Jesus, saw him heal, heard him teach, watched him die, met him arisen, and saw him ascend. John knew God—he had lived with him and had seen him work. And John enjoyed fellowship with the Father and the Son all the days of his life.

The elder statesman in the church, John wrote this letter to his "dear children." In it he presented God as light, as love, and as life. He explained in simple and practical terms what it means to have fellowship with God.

At the same time, false teachers had entered the church, denying the incarnation of Christ. John wrote to correct their serious errors. So John's letter is a model for us to follow as we combat modern heresies.

John opens this letter by presenting his credentials as an eyewitness of the Incarnation and by stating his reason for writing (1:1–4). He then presents God as "light," symbolizing absolute purity and holiness (1:5–7), and he explains how believers can walk in the light and have fellowship with God (1:8–10). If they do sin, Christ is their advocate (2:1, 2). John urges them to obey Christ fully and to love all the members of God's family (2:3–17). He warns his readers of "antichrists" and the Antichrist who will try to lead them away from the truth (2:18–29).

In the next section, John presents God as "love"—giving, dying, forgiving, and blessing (3:1—4:21). God *is* love, and because God loves us, he calls us his children and makes us like Christ (3:1, 2). This truth should motivate us to live close to him (3:3–6). We can be sure of our family relationship with God when our lives are filled with good deeds and love for others (3:7–24). Again, John warns of false teachers who twist the truth. We should reject these false teachers (4:1–6) as we continue to live in God's love (4:7–21).

In the last section, John presents God as "life" (5:1–21). God's life is in his Son. To have his Son is to have eternal life.

Do you know God? Do you know Christ? Do you know that you have eternal life? First John was written to help you know the reality of God in your life through faith in Christ, to assure you that you have eternal life, and to encourage you to remain in fellowship with the God who is light and love. Read this letter written by one overwhelmed by God's love, and with renewed confidence, pass on his love to others.

VITAL STATISTICS

PURPOSE:
To reassure Christians in their faith and to counter false teachings

AUTHOR:
The apostle John

ORIGINAL AUDIENCE:
The letter is untitled and was written to no particular church. It was sent as a pastoral letter to several Gentile congregations.

DATE WRITTEN:
Probably between A.D. 85 and 90 from Ephesus

SETTING:
John was an older man and perhaps the only surviving apostle at this time. He had not yet been banished to the island of Patmos, where he would live in exile. As an eyewitness of Christ, he wrote authoritatively to give this new generation of believers assurance and confidence in God and in their faith.

KEY VERSE:
"I have written this to you who believe in the name of the Son of God, so that you may know you have eternal life" (5:13).

KEY PEOPLE:
John, Jesus

SPECIAL FEATURES:
John is the apostle of love, and love is mentioned throughout this letter. There are a number of similarities between this letter and John's Gospel—in vocabulary, style, and main ideas. John uses brief statements and simple words, and he features sharp contrasts—light and darkness, truth and error, God and Satan, life and death, and love and hate.

THE BLUEPRINT

1. God is light
   (1:1—2:29)
2. God is love
   (3:1—4:21)
3. God is life
   (5:1–21)

John wrote about the most vital aspects of faith so that his readers would know Christian truth from error. He emphasizes the basics of faith so that we can be confident in our faith. In our dark world, God is light. In our cold world, God brings the warmth of love. In our dying world, God brings life. When we lack confidence, these truths bring us certainty.

MEGATHEMES

THEME	EXPLANATION	IMPORTANCE
Sin	Even Christians sin. Sin requires God's forgiveness, and Christ's death provides it for us. Determining to live according to God's standards in the Bible shows that our life is being transformed.	We cannot deny our sin nature, maintain that we are "above" sinning, or minimize the consequences of sin in our relationship with God. We must resist the attraction of sin, yet we must confess when we do sin.
Love	Christ commands us to love others as he loved us. This love is evidence that we are truly saved. God is the Creator of love; he cares that his children love each other.	Love means putting others first and being unselfish. Love is action—showing others we care—not just saying it. To show love we must give sacrificially of our time and money to meet the needs of others.
Family of God	We become God's children by believing in Christ. God's life in us enables us to love our fellow family members.	How we treat others shows who our Father is. Live as a faithful, loving family member.
Truth and Error	Teaching that the physical body does not matter, false teachers encouraged believers to throw off moral restraints. They also taught that Christ wasn't really a man and that we must be saved by having some special mystical knowledge. The result was that people became indifferent to sin.	God is truth and light, so the more we get to know him, the better we can keep focused on the truth. Don't be led astray by any teaching that denies Christ's deity or humanity. Check the message; test the claims.
Assurance	God is in control of heaven and earth. Because his word is true, we can have assurance of eternal life and victory over sin. By faith we can be certain of our eternal destiny with him.	Assurance of our relationship with God is a promise, but it is also a way of life. We build our confidence by trusting in God's Word and in Christ's provision for our sin.

1. God is light
Introduction

1 We proclaim to you the one who existed from the beginning,* whom we have heard and seen. We saw him with our own eyes and touched him with our own hands. He is the Word of life. ²This one who is life itself was revealed to us, and we have seen him. And now we testify and proclaim to you that he is the one who is eternal life. He was with the Father, and then he was revealed to us. ³We proclaim to you what we ourselves have actually seen

1:1
John 1:1, 4, 14
1 Jn 4:14

1:2
John 1:1-4; 19:35;
20:30-31
1 Jn 5:11, 13, 20

1:1 Greek *What was from the beginning.*

• **1:1** First John was written by John, one of Jesus' original 12 disciples. He was probably "the disciple Jesus loved" (John 21:20), and along with Peter and James, he had a special relationship with Jesus. This letter was written between A.D. 85 and 90 from Ephesus, before John's exile to the island of Patmos (see Revelation 1:9). Jerusalem had been destroyed in A.D. 70, and Christians were scattered throughout the empire. By the time John wrote this letter, Christianity had been around for more than a generation. It had faced and survived severe persecution. The main problem confronting the church at this time was declining commitment: Many believers were conforming to the world's standards, failing to stand up for Christ and compromising their faith. False teachers were plentiful, and they were accelerating the church's downward slide away from the Christian faith.

John wrote this letter to put believers back on track, to show the difference between light and darkness (truth and error), and to encourage the church to grow in genuine love for God and for one another. He also wrote to assure true believers that they possessed eternal life and to help them know that their faith was genuine—so they could enjoy all the benefits of being God's children. For more about John, see his Profile in John 13, p. 1783.

• **1:1-5** John opens his first letter to the churches similarly to the way he began his Gospel, emphasizing that Christ ("the Word of life") is eternal, that God came into the world as a human, that he, John, was an eyewitness to Jesus' life. John had lived with Jesus, having personal, physical contact with Jesus. He knew beyond any doubt that Jesus brings light and life.

• **1:3** As an eyewitness to Jesus' ministry, John was qualified to teach the truth about him. The readers of this letter had not seen and heard Jesus themselves, but they could trust that what John wrote was accurate. We are like those second- and third-generation Christians. Though we have not personally seen, heard, or touched Jesus, we have the New Testament record of his eyewitnesses, and we can trust that they spoke the truth about him. See John 20:29.

1:3, 4 John writes about having fellowship with other believers. There are three principles behind true Christian fellowship:

1:4
John 15:11; 16:24

and heard so that you may have fellowship with us. And our fellowship is with the Father and with his Son, Jesus Christ. ⁴We are writing these things so that you may fully share our joy.*

Living in the Light

1:5
John 1:9; 8:12
1 Tim 6:16

1:6
John 3:19-21
2 Cor 6:14

1:7
Heb 9:14

⁵This is the message we heard from Jesus* and now declare to you: God is light, and there is no darkness in him at all. ⁶So we are lying if we say we have fellowship with God but go on living in spiritual darkness; we are not practicing the truth. ⁷But if we are living in the light, as God is in the light, then we have fellowship with each other, and the blood of Jesus, his Son, cleanses us from all sin.

⁸If we claim we have no sin, we are only fooling ourselves and not living in the truth.

1:4 Or *so that our joy may be complete;* some manuscripts read *your joy.*   1:5 Greek *from him.*

JOHN COUNTERS FALSE TEACHINGS

John counters two major threads in the false teachings of the heretics in this letter:

1:6, 8, 10 . . . . They denied the reality of sin. John says that if we continue in sin, we can't claim to belong to God. If we say we have no sin, we are only fooling ourselves and refusing to live according to the truth.

2:22; 4:1-3 . . . . They denied that Jesus was the Messiah—God in the flesh. John said that if we believe that Jesus was God incarnate and trust him for our salvation, we are children of God.

First, our fellowship is grounded in the testimony of God's Word. Without this underlying strength, togetherness is impossible. Second, it is mutual, depending on the unity of believers. Third, it is renewed daily through the Holy Spirit. True fellowship combines social and spiritual interaction, and it is made possible only through a living relationship with Christ.

● **1:5, 6** Light represents what is good, pure, true, holy, and reliable. Darkness represents what is sinful and evil. The statement "God is light" means that God is perfectly holy and true and that he alone can guide us out of the darkness of sin. Light is also related to truth in that light exposes whatever exists, whether it is good or bad. In the dark, good and evil look alike; in the light, they can be clearly distinguished. Just as darkness cannot exist in the presence of light, sin cannot exist in the presence of a holy God. If we want to have a relationship with God, we must put aside our sinful ways of living. To claim that we belong to him but then to go out and live for ourselves is hypocrisy. Christ will expose and judge such deceit.

● **1:6** Here John was confronting the first of three claims of the false teachers: that we can have fellowship with God and go on living in spiritual darkness. False teachers who thought that the physical body was evil or worthless taught one of two approaches to behavior: They insisted on denying bodily desires through rigid discipline, or they approved of gratifying every physical lust because the body was going to be destroyed anyway. Obviously the second approach was more popular! Here John is saying that no one can claim to be a Christian and still live in evil and immorality. We can't love God and court sin at the same time.

● **1:7** How does Jesus' blood cleanse us from all sin? In Old Testament times, believers symbolically transferred their sins to an animal, which they then sacrificed (see a description of this ceremony in Leviticus 4). The animal died in their place to pay for their sin and to allow them to continue living in God's favor. God graciously forgave them because of their faith in him and because they obeyed his commandments concerning the sacrifice. Those sacrifices anticipated the day when Christ would completely remove sin. Real cleansing from sin came with Jesus, "the Lamb of God who takes away the sin of the world" (John 1:29). Sin, by its very nature, brings death—that is a fact as certain as the law of gravity. Jesus did not die for his own sins; he had none. Instead, by a transaction that we may never fully understand, he died for the sins of the world. When we commit our life to Christ and thus identify

ourselves with him, his death becomes ours. He has paid the penalty for our sins, and his blood has purified us. Just as Christ rose from the grave, we rise to a new life of fellowship with him (Romans 6:4).

● **1:8** Here John was attacking the second claim of the false teachers: that people had no natural tendency toward sin, that they had "no sin," and that they were then incapable of sinning. This is a lie. The false teachers refused to take sin seriously. They wanted to be considered Christians, but they saw no need to confess and repent. The death of Christ did not mean much to them because they didn't think they needed it. Instead of repenting and being purified by Christ's blood, they were encouraging sin among believers. In this life we are always capable of sinning, so we should never let down our guard.

● **1:8-10** The false teachers not only denied that sin breaks fellowship with God (1:6) and that they had a sinful nature (1:8), but they also denied that their conduct involved any sin at all (1:10). That was a lie that ignored one basic truth: All people are sinners by nature and by practice. At conversion all our sins are forgiven—past, present, and future. Yet even after we become Christians, we still sin and still need to confess. This kind of confession is not offered to gain God's acceptance but to remove the barrier to fellowship that our sin has put between us and him. It is difficult, however, for many people to admit their faults and shortcomings, even to God. It takes humility and honesty to recognize our weaknesses, and most of us would rather pretend that we are strong. But we need not fear revealing our sins to God—he knows them already. He will not push us away, no matter what we've done. Instead, he will draw us to himself.

⁹But if we confess our sins to him, he is faithful and just to forgive us our sins and to cleanse us from all wickedness. ¹⁰If we claim we have not sinned, we are calling God a liar and showing that his word has no place in our hearts.

1:9
Heb 9:14
1:10
1 Jn 5:10

2 My dear children, I am writing this to you so that you will not sin. But if anyone does sin, we have an advocate who pleads our case before the Father. He is Jesus Christ, the one who is truly righteous. ²He himself is the sacrifice that atones for our sins—and not only our sins but the sins of all the world.

³And we can be sure that we know him if we obey his commandments. ⁴If someone claims, "I know God," but doesn't obey God's commandments, that person is a liar and is not living in the truth. ⁵But those who obey God's word truly show how completely they love him. That is how we know we are living in him. ⁶Those who say they live in God should live their lives as Jesus did.

2:1
1 Tim 2:5
Heb 7:25; 9:24
2:2
John 1:29
Rom 3:25
Heb 2:17
1 Jn 4:10
2:5
John 14:21, 23
2:6
Matt 11:29
John 13:15
1 Pet 2:21

A New Commandment

⁷Dear friends, I am not writing a new commandment for you; rather it is an old one you have had from the very beginning. This old commandment—to love one another—is the same message you heard before. ⁸Yet it is also new. Jesus lived the truth of this commandment, and you also are living it. For the darkness is disappearing, and the true light is already shining.

⁹If anyone claims, "I am living in the light," but hates a Christian brother or sister,* that

2:7
John 13:34
2 Jn 1:5-6
2:8
John 1:9; 13:34
Rom 13:12
Eph 5:8
1 Thes 5:5

2:9 Greek *hates his brother;* similarly in 2:11.

● **1:9** Confession is supposed to free us to enjoy fellowship with Christ. It should ease our consciences and lighten our cares. But some Christians do not understand how it works. They feel so guilty that they confess the same sins over and over; then they wonder if they might have forgotten something. Other Christians believe that God forgives them when they confess, but if they died with unconfessed sins, they would be forever lost. These Christians do not understand that God *wants* to forgive us. He allowed his beloved Son to die just so he could offer us pardon. When we come to Christ, he forgives all the sins we have committed or will ever commit. We don't need to confess the sins of the past all over again, and we don't need to fear that God will reject us if we don't keep our slate perfectly clean. Of course we should continue to confess our sins, but not because failure to do so will make us lose our salvation. Our relationship with Christ is secure. Instead, we should confess so that we can enjoy maximum fellowship and joy with him.

True confession also involves a commitment not to continue in sin. We wouldn't be genuinely confessing our sins to God if we planned to commit them again and just wanted temporary forgiveness. We should also pray for strength to defeat temptation the next time we face it.

● **1:9** If God has forgiven us for our sins because of Christ's death, why must we confess our sins? In admitting our sins and receiving Christ's cleansing, we are (1) agreeing with God that our sin truly is sin and that we are willing to turn from it, (2) ensuring that we don't conceal our sins from him and consequently from ourselves, and (3) recognizing our tendency to sin and relying on his power to overcome it.

2:1 John uses "dear children" in a warm, fatherly way. He is not talking down to his readers but is showing affection for them. At this writing, John was a very old man. He had spent almost all his life in ministry, and many of his readers were indeed his spiritual children.

● **2:1, 2** To people who are feeling guilty and condemned, John offers reassurance. They know they have sinned, and Satan (called "the accuser" in Revelation 12:10) is demanding the death penalty. When you feel this way, don't give up hope—the best defense attorney in the universe is pleading your case. Jesus Christ, your advocate, your defender, is the Judge's Son. He has already suffered your penalty in your place. You can't be tried for a case that is no longer on the docket. United with Christ, you are as safe as he is. Don't be afraid to ask Christ to plead your case—he has already won it (see Romans 8:33, 34; Hebrews 7:24, 25).

● **2:2** Jesus Christ is the atoning sacrifice for our sins (see also 4:10). He is our defense attorney. He can stand before God as our mediator because his death satisfied the wrath of God against sin and paid the death penalty for our sin. Thus, Christ both satisfies God's requirement and removes our sin. In him we are forgiven and purified.

2:2 Sometimes it is difficult to forgive those who wrong us. Imagine how hard it would be to forgive all people, no matter what they had done! This is what God has done in Jesus. No one, no matter what sin has been committed, is beyond forgiveness. All a person has to do is turn from sin, receive Christ's forgiveness, and commit his or her life to him.

● **2:3-6** How can you be sure that you belong to Christ? This passage gives two ways to know: if you do what Christ says and live as Christ wants. What does Christ tell us to do? John answers in 3:23: "Believe in the name of his Son, Jesus Christ, and love one another." True Christian faith results in loving behavior; that is why John says that the way we act can give us assurance that we belong to Christ.

● **2:6** To live as Jesus lived doesn't mean choosing 12 disciples, performing great miracles, and being crucified. We cannot merely copy Christ's life; much of what Jesus did had to do with his identity as God's Son, the fulfillment of his special role in dying for sin, and the cultural context of the first-century Roman world. To walk today as Christ did, we must obey his teachings and follow his example of complete obedience to God and loving service to people.

● **2:7, 8** The commandment to love others is both old and new. It is old because it comes from the Old Testament (Leviticus 19:18). It is new because Jesus interpreted it in a radically new way (John 13:34, 35). In the Christian church, love is not only expressed by showing respect; it is also expressed through self-sacrifice and servanthood (John 15:13). In fact, it can be defined as "selfless giving," reaching beyond friends to enemies and persecutors (Matthew 5:43-48). Love should be the unifying force and the identifying mark of the Christian community. Love is the key to walking in the light, because we cannot grow spiritually while we hate others. Our growing relationship with God will result in growing relationships with others.

● **2:9-11** Does this mean that if you dislike someone you aren't a Christian? These verses are not talking about disliking a disagreeable Christian brother or sister. There will always be people we will not like as well as others. John's words focus on the attitude that causes us to ignore or despise others, to treat them as

2:10
Rom 14:13

2:11
John 12:35
2 Cor 4:4
2 Pet 1:9
1 Jn 2:9; 3:15

2:12
1 Cor 6:11

2:13
John 1:1; 16:33
1 Jn 1:1; 4:4; 5:18

2:14
John 1:1-2
Eph 6:10
1 Jn 1:1; 1:10

person is still living in darkness. ¹⁰Anyone who loves another brother or sister* is living in the light and does not cause others to stumble. ¹¹But anyone who hates another brother or sister is still living and walking in darkness. Such a person does not know the way to go, having been blinded by the darkness.

¹² I am writing to you who are God's children
    because your sins have been forgiven through Jesus.*
¹³ I am writing to you who are mature in the faith*
    because you know Christ, who existed from the beginning.
I am writing to you who are young in the faith
    because you have won your battle with the evil one.
¹⁴ I have written to you who are God's children
    because you know the Father.
I have written to you who are mature in the faith
    because you know Christ, who existed from the beginning.
I have written to you who are young in the faith
    because you are strong.
God's word lives in your hearts,
    and you have won your battle with the evil one.

2:15
Rom 12:2
Jas 4:4

2:16
Rom 13:14
Eph 2:3

Do Not Love This World

¹⁵Do not love this world nor the things it offers you, for when you love the world, you do not have the love of the Father in you. ¹⁶For the world offers only a craving for physical

2:10 Greek *loves his brother.* **2:12** Greek *through his name.* **2:13** Or *to you fathers;* also in 2:14.

A BOOK OF CONTRASTS

One of the distinct features of John's willing style was his habit of noting both sides of a conflict. He wrote to show the difference between real Christianity and anything else. Here are some of his favorite contrasts.

Contrast between	Passage
Light and darkness	1:5
The new commandment and the old commandment.	2:7, 8
Loving the Father and loving the world	2:15, 16
Christ and Antichrist	2:18, 22
Truth and lies	2:20, 21
Children of God and children of the devil	3:1-10
Eternal life and eternal death	3:14
Love and hatred.	3:15, 16
True prophecy and false prophecy	4:1-3
Love and fear.	4:18, 19
Having life and not having life	5:11, 12

---

irritants, competitors, or enemies. Christian love is not a feeling but a choice. We can choose to be concerned with people's well being and treat them with respect, whether or not we feel affection toward them. If we choose to love others, God will help us express our love.

2:12-14 John was writing to believers of all ages. The "children" had experienced forgiveness through Jesus. Those who were "mature in the faith" had a long-standing relationship with Christ. The "young in the faith" had battled with Satan's temptations and had won. Each stage of life in the Christian pilgrimage builds upon the other. As children learn about Christ, they grow in their ability to win battles with temptation. As young adults move from victory to victory, they grow in their relationship with Christ. Older adults, having known Christ for years, have developed the wisdom needed to teach young people and start the cycle all over again. Has your Christian growth reached the maturity level appropriate for your stage in life?

• **2:15, 16** Some people think that worldliness is limited to external behavior—the people we associate with, the places we go,

the activities we enjoy. Worldliness is also internal because it begins in the heart and is characterized by three attitudes: (1) *craving for physical pleasure*—preoccupation with gratifying physical desires; (2) *craving for everything we see*—coveting and accumulating things, bowing to the god of materialism; and (3) *pride in our achievements and possessions*—obsession with one's status or importance. When the serpent tempted Eve (Genesis 3:6), he tempted her in these areas. Also, when the devil tempted Jesus in the wilderness, these were his three areas of attack (see Matthew 4:1-11).

By contrast, God values self-control, a spirit of generosity, and a commitment to humble service. It is possible to give the impression of avoiding worldly pleasures while still harboring worldly attitudes in one's heart. It is also possible, like Jesus, to love sinners and spend time with them while maintaining a commitment to the values of God's Kingdom. What values are most important to you? Do your actions reflect the world's values or God's values?

pleasure, a craving for everything we see, and pride in our achievements and possessions. These are not from the Father, but are from this world. ¹⁷And this world is fading away, along with everything that people crave. But anyone who does what pleases God will live forever.

2:17
Matt 7:21
1 Cor 7:31

Warning about Antichrists

¹⁸Dear children, the last hour is here. You have heard that the Antichrist is coming, and already many such antichrists have appeared. From this we know that the last hour has come. ¹⁹These people left our churches, but they never really belonged with us; otherwise they would have stayed with us. When they left, it proved that they did not belong with us.

2:18
Matt 24:24

2:19
Acts 20:30
1 Cor 11:19

²⁰But you are not like that, for the Holy One has given you his Spirit,* and all of you know the truth. ²¹So I am writing to you not because you don't know the truth but because you know the difference between truth and lies. ²²And who is a liar? Anyone who says that Jesus is not the Christ.* Anyone who denies the Father and the Son is an antichrist.* ²³Anyone who denies the Son doesn't have the Father, either. But anyone who acknowledges the Son has the Father also.

2:22
1 Jn 4:3

2:23
John 8:19; 17:3
1 Jn 4:15; 5:1

²⁴So you must remain faithful to what you have been taught from the beginning. If you do, you will remain in fellowship with the Son and with the Father. ²⁵And in this fellowship we enjoy the eternal life he promised us.

2:24
1 Jn 4:15; 5:1
2 Jn 1:9

2:25
John 3:15; 6:40;
17:3

²⁶I am writing these things to warn you about those who want to lead you astray. ²⁷But you have received the Holy Spirit,* and he lives within you, so you don't need anyone to teach you what is true. For the Spirit* teaches you everything you need to know, and what he teaches is true—it is not a lie. So just as he has taught you, remain in fellowship with Christ.

2:27
John 14:16, 26;
16:13
1 Cor 2:10-12

2:20 Greek *But you have an anointing from the Holy One.*   **2:22a** Or *not the Messiah.*   **2:22b** Or *the antichrist.*
2:27a Greek *the anointing from him.*   **2:27b** Greek *the anointing.*

• **2:17** When the desire for possessions and sinful pleasures feels so intense, we probably doubt that these objects of desire will all one day pass away. It may be even more difficult to believe that the person who does the will of God will live forever. But this was John's conviction based on the facts of Jesus' life, death, resurrection, and promises. Knowing that this evil world will end can give you the courage to deny yourself temporary pleasures in this world in order to enjoy what God has promised for eternity.

• **2:18-23** John is talking about the last days, the time between Christ's first and second comings. The first-century readers of 1 John lived in the last days, and so do we. During this time, antichrists (false teachers who pretend to be Christians and who lure weak members away from Christ) will appear. Finally, just before the world ends, one great Antichrist will arise (Revelation 13; 19:20; 20:10). We do not need to fear these evil people, however. The Holy Spirit shows us their errors, so we will not be deceived. However, we must teach God's Word clearly and carefully to the peripheral, weak members among us so that they won't fall prey to these teachers who "come disguised as harmless sheep but are really vicious wolves" (Matthew 7:15).

• **2:19** The antichrists were not total strangers to the church; they once had been in the church, but they did not really belong to it. John does not say why they left; it is clear that their reasons for joining in the first place were wrong. Some people may call themselves Christians for less than the best reasons. Perhaps going to church is a family tradition. Maybe they like the social and business contacts they make there. Or possibly going to church is a long-standing habit, and they have never stopped to ask themselves why they do it. What is your main reason for being a Christian? Unless it is a Christ-centered reason, you may not really belong. You don't have to settle for less than the best. You can become personally acquainted with Jesus Christ and become a loyal, trustworthy follower.

• **2:20** When a person becomes a Christian, he or she receives the Holy Spirit. One way the Holy Spirit helps the believer and the church is by communicating truth. Jesus is the truth (John 14:6), and the Holy Spirit guides believers to him (John 16:13). People who are opposed to Christ are also opposed to his truth, and the Holy Spirit is not working in their lives. When we are led by the Spirit, we can stand against false teachers and the Antichrist. Ask the Spirit to guide you each day (see 2:27).

• **2:22, 23** Apparently the antichrists in John's day were claiming faith in God while denying and opposing Christ. To do so, John firmly states, is impossible. Because Jesus is God's Son and the Messiah, to deny Christ is to reject God's way of revealing himself to the world. A person who accepts Christ as God's Son, however, accepts God the Father at the same time. The two are one and cannot be separated. Many cultists today call themselves Christians, but they deny that Jesus is divine. We must expose these heresies and oppose such teachings so that the weak believers among us do not succumb to their teachings.

• **2:24** These Christians had heard the Good News, very likely from John himself. They knew that Christ was God's Son, that he died for their sins and was raised to give them new life, and that he would return and establish his Kingdom in its fullness. But their fellowship was being infiltrated by teachers who denied these basic doctrines of the Christian faith, and some of the believers were in danger of succumbing to false arguments. John encouraged them to hold on to the Christian truth they heard at the beginning of their walk with Christ. It is important to grow in our knowledge of the Lord, to deepen our understanding through careful study, and to teach these truths to others. But no matter how much we learn, we must never abandon the basic truths about Christ. Jesus will always be God's Son, and his sacrifice for our sins is permanent. No truth will ever contradict these teachings in the Bible.

• **2:26, 27** Christ had promised to send the Holy Spirit to teach his followers and to remind them of all that Christ had taught (John 14:26). As a result, Christians have the Holy Spirit within them to keep them from going astray. In addition, they have the God-inspired Scriptures, against which they can test questionable teachings. To stay true to Christ, we must follow his Word and his Spirit. Let the Holy Spirit help you discern truth from error. For more about who the Holy Spirit is and what he does, see the notes on John 3:6, Acts 1:5, and Ephesians 1:13, 14.

2:27 Christ lives in us through the Holy Spirit, and we also live in Christ. This means that we place our total trust in him, rely on him for guidance and strength, and live as he wants us to live.

2:28
Col 3:4
1 Thes 2:19
1 Jn 3:2, 21

2:29
1 Jn 3:7, 10; 4:7

28And now, dear children, remain in fellowship with Christ so that when he returns, you will be full of courage and not shrink back from him in shame.

29Since we know that Christ is righteous, we also know that all who do what is right are God's children.

2. God is love

Living as Children of God

3:1
John 1:12-13; 16:3;
17:26
Rom 8:16
Eph 1:4-5

3:2
John 17:24
Rom 8:19, 29
2 Cor 3:18
Phil 3:21

3:4
Matt 7:23

3:5
Isa 53:1-12
John 1:29
2 Cor 5:21

3:6
Rom 6:14
1 Jn 3:9

3:8
John 8:44

3:9
Jas 1:18
1 Pet 1:3

3:10
John 1:12-13

3 See how very much our Father loves us, for he calls us his children, and that is what we are! But the people who belong to this world don't recognize that we are God's children because they don't know him. 2Dear friends, we are already God's children, but he has not yet shown us what we will be like when Christ appears. But we do know that we will be like him, for we will see him as he really is. 3And all who have this eager expectation will keep themselves pure, just as he is pure.

4Everyone who sins is breaking God's law, for all sin is contrary to the law of God. 5And you know that Jesus came to take away our sins, and there is no sin in him. 6Anyone who continues to live in him will not sin. But anyone who keeps on sinning does not know him or understand who he is.

7Dear children, don't let anyone deceive you about this: When people do what is right, it shows that they are righteous, even as Christ is righteous. 8But when people keep on sinning, it shows that they belong to the devil, who has been sinning since the beginning. But the Son of God came to destroy the works of the devil. 9Those who have been born into God's family do not make a practice of sinning, because God's life* is in them. So they can't keep on sinning, because they are children of God. 10So now we can tell who are children of God and who are children of the devil. Anyone who does not live righteously and does not love other believers* does not belong to God.

3:9 Greek *because his seed.*   **3:10** Greek *does not love his brother.*

It implies a personal, life-giving relationship. John uses the same idea in John 15:5, where he speaks of Christ as the vine and his followers as the branches (see also 3:24; 4:15).

• **2:28, 29** The visible proof of being a Christian is right behavior. Many people do good deeds but don't have faith in Jesus Christ. Others claim to have faith but rarely produce good deeds. A deficit in either faith or right behavior will be a cause for shame when Christ returns. Because true faith always results in good deeds, those who claim to have faith *and* who consistently do what is right are true believers. Good deeds cannot produce salvation (see Ephesians 2:8, 9), but they are necessary proof that true faith is actually present (James 2:14-17).

3:1 As believers, our self-worth is based on the fact that God loves us and calls us his children. We are his children *now,* not just sometime in the distant future. Knowing that we are his children should encourage us to live as Jesus did. For other references about being part of God's family, see Romans 8:14-17; Galatians 3:26, 27; 4:6, 7.

3:1ff Verse 1 tells us who we are—members of God's family, his children. Verse 2 tells us who we are becoming—reflections of God. The rest of the chapter tells us what we have as we grow to resemble God: (1) victory over sin (3:4-9); (2) love for others (3:10-18); and (3) confidence before God (3:19-24).

• **3:2, 3** The Christian life is a process of becoming more and more like Christ (see Romans 8:29). This process will not be complete until we see Christ face to face (1 Corinthians 13:12; Philippians 3:21), but knowing that it is our ultimate destiny should motivate us to purify ourselves. To keep pure means to keep morally straight, free from the corruption of sin. God also purifies us, but there is action we must take to remain morally fit (see 1 Timothy 5:22; James 4:8; 1 Peter 1:22).

• **3:4ff** There is a difference between committing a sin and continuing to sin. Even the most faithful believers sometimes commit sins, but they do not cherish a particular sin or continually choose to commit it. A believer who commits a sin can repent, confess it, and find forgiveness. A person who continues to sin, by contrast, is not sorry for what he or she is doing. Thus, this person never confesses and never receives forgiveness. Such a

person is in opposition to God, no matter what religious claims he or she makes.

• **3:5** Under the Old Testament sacrifice system, a lamb without blemish was offered as a sacrifice for sin. Jesus is "the Lamb of God who takes away the sin of the world" (John 1:29). Because Jesus lived a perfect life and sacrificed himself for our sins, we can be completely forgiven (2:2). We can look back to his death for us and know that we need never suffer eternal death (1 Peter 1:18-20).

• **3:8, 9** We all have areas where temptation is strong and habits are hard to conquer. These weaknesses give the devil a foothold, so we must deal with our areas of vulnerability. If we are struggling with a particular sin, however, these verses are not directed at us, even if for the time we seem to keep on sinning. John is not talking about people whose victories are still incomplete; he is talking about people who make a practice of sinning and look for ways to justify it.

Three steps are necessary to find victory over prevailing sin: (1) Seek the power of the Holy Spirit and God's Word; (2) stay away from tempting situations; and (3) seek the help of the body of Christ—be open to their willingness to hold you accountable and to pray for you.

• **3:9** "They can't keep on sinning" means that true believers do not make a practice of sinning, nor do they become indifferent to God's moral law. All believers still sin, but they are working to gain victory over sin.

• **3:9** We are "born into God's family" when the Holy Spirit lives in us and gives us Jesus' new life. Being born again is more than a fresh start; it is a rebirth, receiving a new family name based on Christ's death for us. When this happens, God forgives us and totally accepts us; the Holy Spirit gives us a new mind and heart, lives in us, and begins helping us to become like Christ. Our perspective changes, too, because we have a mind that is renewed day by day by the Holy Spirit (see Romans 12:2; Ephesians 4:22-24). So we must begin to think and act differently. See John 3:1-21 for more on being born again.

Love One Another

¹¹This is the message you have heard from the beginning: We should love one another. ¹²We must not be like Cain, who belonged to the evil one and killed his brother. And why did he kill him? Because Cain had been doing what was evil, and his brother had been doing what was righteous. ¹³So don't be surprised, dear brothers and sisters,* if the world hates you.

¹⁴If we love our Christian brothers and sisters,* it proves that we have passed from death to life. But a person who has no love is still dead. ¹⁵Anyone who hates another brother or sister* is really a murderer at heart. And you know that murderers don't have eternal life within them.

¹⁶We know what real love is because Jesus gave up his life for us. So we also ought to give up our lives for our brothers and sisters. ¹⁷If someone has enough money to live well and sees a brother or sister* in need but shows no compassion—how can God's love be in that person?

¹⁸Dear children, let's not merely say that we love each other; let us show the truth by our actions. ¹⁹Our actions will show that we belong to the truth, so we will be confident when we stand before God. ²⁰Even if we feel guilty, God is greater than our feelings, and he knows everything.

²¹Dear friends, if we don't feel guilty, we can come to God with bold confidence. ²²And we will receive from him whatever we ask because we obey him and do the things that please him.

²³And this is his commandment: We must believe in the name of his Son, Jesus Christ, and love one another, just as he commanded us. ²⁴Those who obey God's commandments remain in fellowship with him, and he with them. And we know he lives in us because the Spirit he gave us lives in us.

Discerning False Prophets

4 Dear friends, do not believe everyone who claims to speak by the Spirit. You must test them to see if the spirit they have comes from God. For there are many false prophets in the world. ²This is how we know if they have the Spirit of God: If a person claiming to be a prophet* acknowledges that Jesus Christ came in a real body, that person has the Spirit of

3:11
John 13:34; 15:12

3:12
Gen 4:3-8

3:13
John 15:18

3:15
Matt 5:21-22
John 8:44

3:16
John 13:1; 15:13
Phil 2:17

3:17
Deut 15:7-8
Jas 2:15

3:18
Rom 12:9
Jas 1:22

3:19
John 18:37

3:21
Rom 5:1

3:22
Matt 7:7
John 8:29; 14:13

3:23
John 6:29; 13:34

3:24
Rom 8:9

4:1
1 Thes 5:21
1 Jn 2:18

4:2
John 1:14
1 Cor 12:3

3:13 Greek *brothers.*   **3:14** Greek *the brothers;* similarly in 3:16.   **3:15** Greek *hates his brother.*   **3:17** Greek *sees his brother.*   **4:2** Greek *If a spirit;* similarly in 4:3.

3:12, 13 Cain killed his brother, Abel, when God accepted Abel's offering and not his (Genesis 4:1-16). Abel's offering showed that Cain was not giving his best to God, and Cain's jealous anger drove him to murder. People who are morally upright expose and shame those who aren't. If we live for God, the world will often hate us, because we make them painfully aware of their immoral way of living.

• **3:15** John echoes Jesus' teaching that whoever hates another person is a murderer at heart (Matthew 5:21, 22). Christianity is a religion of the heart; outward compliance alone is not enough. Bitterness against someone who has wronged you is an evil cancer within you and will eventually destroy you. Don't let a "poisonous root of bitterness" (Hebrews 12:15) grow in you or your church.

• **3:16** Real love is an action, not a feeling. It produces selfless, sacrificial giving. The greatest act of love is giving oneself for others. How can we "give up our lives"? By serving others with no thought of receiving anything in return. Sometimes it is easier to say we'll die for others than to truly live for them—this involves putting others' desires first. Jesus taught this same principle of love in John 15:13.

• **3:17, 18** These verses give an example of how to give up our life for others—to help those in need. This is strikingly similar to James's teaching (James 2:14-17). How clearly do your actions say you really love others? Are you as generous as you should be with your money, possessions, and time?

• **3:19, 20** Many are afraid that they don't love others as they should. They feel guilty because they think they are not doing enough to show proper love to Christ. Their consciences bother them. John has these people in mind in this letter. How do we escape the gnawing accusations of our consciences? Not by ignoring them or rationalizing our behavior but by setting our heart on God's love. When we feel guilty, we should remind ourselves that God knows our motives as well as our actions. His voice of assurance is stronger than the accusing voice of our conscience. If we are in Christ, he will not condemn us (Romans 8:1; Hebrews 9:14, 15). So if you are living for the Lord but feeling that you are not good enough, remind yourself that God is greater than your conscience.

3:21, 22 If your conscience is clear, you can come to God without fear, confident that your requests will be heard. John reaffirms Jesus' promise that whatever we ask for will be given to us (Matthew 7:7; see also Matthew 21:22; John 9:31; 15:7). You will receive if you obey and do what pleases him because you will then be asking in line with God's will. Of course this does not mean that you can have anything you want, like instant riches. If you are truly seeking God's will, there are some requests you will not make.

• **3:23** In the Bible, a person's name stands for his or her character. It represents who he or she really is. We are to believe not only in Jesus' words, but also in his very person as the Son of God. Moreover, to believe "in the name" means to pattern your life after Christ's, to become more like him by uniting yourself with him. And if we are living like Christ, we will "love one another."

• **3:24** The mutual relationship, living in Christ as he lives in us, shows itself in Christians who keep these three essential commands: (1) Believe in Christ, (2) love the brothers and sisters, and (3) live morally upright lives. The Spirit's presence is not only spiritual and mystical, but it is also practical. Our conduct verifies his presence.

• **4:1, 2** "Do not believe everyone who claims to speak by the Spirit. You must test them to see if the spirit they have comes from God" means that we shouldn't believe everything we hear just because someone says it is a message from God. There are many ways to test teachers to see if their message is truly from the Lord. One is to check to see if their words match what God

4:3
2 Jn 1:7

4:4
John 12:31
Rom 8:31
1 Jn 2:1

4:5
John 15:19;
17:14, 16

4:6
John 8:47; 14:17
1 Cor 14:37
1 Tim 4:1

God. 3But if someone claims to be a prophet and does not acknowledge the truth about Jesus, that person is not from God. Such a person has the spirit of the Antichrist, which you heard is coming into the world and indeed is already here.

4But you belong to God, my dear children. You have already won a victory over those people, because the Spirit who lives in you is greater than the spirit who lives in the world. 5Those people belong to this world, so they speak from the world's viewpoint, and the world listens to them. 6But we belong to God, and those who know God listen to us. If they do not belong to God, they do not listen to us. That is how we know if someone has the Spirit of truth or the spirit of deception.

Loving One Another

4:7
1 Jn 2:29; 3:11; 4:9
John 3:16

7Dear friends, let us continue to love one another, for love comes from God. Anyone who loves is a child of God and knows God. 8But anyone who does not love does not know God, for God is love.

HERESIES

Most of the eyewitnesses to Jesus' ministry had died by the time John composed this letter. Some of the second- or third-generation Christians began to have doubts about what they had been taught about Jesus. Some Christians with a Greek background had a hard time believing that Jesus was human as well as divine, because in Platonic thought the spirit was all-important. The body was only a prison from which one desired to escape. Heresies developed from a uniting of this kind of Platonic thought and Christianity.

A particularly widespread false teaching, later called *Docetism* (from a Greek word meaning "to seem"), held that Jesus was actually a spirit who only appeared to have a body. In reality he cast no shadow and left no footprints; he was God but not man. Another heretical teaching, related to *Gnosticism* (from a Greek word meaning "knowledge", held that all physical matter was evil, the spirit was good, and only the intellectually enlightened could enjoy the benefits of religion. Both groups found it hard to believe in a Savior who was fully human.

John answers these false teachers as an eyewitness to Jesus' life on earth. He saw Jesus, talked with him, touched him—he knew that Jesus was more than a mere spirit. In the very first sentence of his letter, John establishes that Jesus had been alive before the world began and also that he lived as a man among men and women. In other words, he was both divine and human.

Through the centuries, many heretics have denied that Jesus was both God and man. In John's day people had trouble believing he was human; today more people have problems seeing him as God. But Jesus' divine-human nature is the pivotal issue of Christianity. Before you accept what religious teachers say about any topic, listen carefully to what they believe about Jesus. To deny either his divinity or his humanity is to consider him less than Christ, the Savior.

---

says in the Bible. Other tests include their commitment to the body of believers (2:19), their life-styles (3:23, 24), and the fruit of their ministries (4:6). But the most important test of all, says John, is what they believe about Christ. Do they teach that Jesus is fully God and fully man? Our world is filled with voices claiming to speak for God. Give them these tests to see if they are indeed speaking God's truth.

4:3 The Antichrist will be a person who epitomizes all that is evil, and he will be readily received by an evil world. He is more fully described in 2 Thessalonians 2:3-12 and Revelation 13. The "spirit of the Antichrist" is already here (see the note on 2:18-23). Those who reject Christ are unknowingly or consciously siding with the spirit of the Antichrist.

4:4 It is easy to be frightened by the wickedness we see all around us and to be overwhelmed by the problems we face. Evil is obviously much stronger than we are. John assures us, however, that God is even stronger. He will conquer all evil—and his Spirit and his Word live in our heart!

• **4:6** False teachers are popular with the world because, like the false prophets of the Old Testament, they tell people what they want to hear. John warns that Christians who faithfully teach God's Word will not win any popularity contests in the world. People don't want to hear their sins denounced; they don't want to listen to demands that they change their behavior. A false teacher will be well received by non-Christians.

• **4:7ff** Everyone believes that love is important, but love is usually thought of as a feeling. In reality, love is a choice and an action, as 1 Corinthians 13:4-7 shows. God is the source of our love. He loved us enough to sacrifice his Son for us. Jesus is our example of what it means to love; everything he did in life and death was supremely loving. The Holy Spirit gives us the power to love; he lives in our heart and makes us more and more like Christ. God's love always involves a choice and an action, and our love should be like his. How well do you display your love for God in the choices you make and the actions you take?

• **4:8** John says, "God is love," not "Love is God." Our world, with its shallow and selfish view of love, has turned these words around and contaminated our understanding of love. The world thinks that love is what makes a person feel good and that it is all right to sacrifice moral principles and others' rights in order to obtain such "love." But that isn't real love; it is the exact opposite—selfishness. And God is not that kind of "love." Real love is like God, who is holy, just, and perfect. If we truly know God, we will love as he does.

⁹God showed how much he loved us by sending his one and only Son into the world so that we might have eternal life through him. ¹⁰This is real love—not that we loved God, but that he loved us and sent his Son as a sacrifice to take away our sins.

¹¹Dear friends, since God loved us that much, we surely ought to love each other. ¹²No one has ever seen God. But if we love each other, God lives in us, and his love is brought to full expression in us.

¹³And God has given us his Spirit as proof that we live in him and he in us. ¹⁴Furthermore, we have seen with our own eyes and now testify that the Father sent his Son to be the Savior of the world. ¹⁵All who confess that Jesus is the Son of God have God living in them, and they live in God. ¹⁶We know how much God loves us, and we have put our trust in his love.

God is love, and all who live in love live in God, and God lives in them. ¹⁷And as we live in God, our love grows more perfect. So we will not be afraid on the day of judgment, but we can face him with confidence because we live like Jesus here in this world.

¹⁸Such love has no fear, because perfect love expels all fear. If we are afraid, it is for fear of punishment, and this shows that we have not fully experienced his perfect love. ¹⁹We love each other* because he loved us first.

²⁰If someone says, "I love God," but hates a Christian brother or sister,* that person is a liar; for if we don't love people we can see, how can we love God, whom we cannot see? ²¹And he has given us this command: Those who love God must also love their Christian brothers and sisters.*

3. God is life

Faith in the Son of God

5 Everyone who believes that Jesus is the Christ* has become a child of God. And everyone who loves the Father loves his children, too. ²We know we love God's children if we love God and obey his commandments. ³Loving God means keeping his commandments,

4:19 Greek *We love.* Other manuscripts read *We love God;* still others read *We love him.* **4:20** Greek *hates his brother.* **4:21** Greek *The one who loves God must also love his brother.* **5:1** Or *the Messiah.*

4:10
Rom 5:8, 10
1 Jn 2:2

4:11
Matt 18:33

4:12
John 1:18; 14:23
1 Tim 6:16

4:13
Rom 8:9
1 Jn 3:24

4:14
John 1:14; 3:17;
4:42
1 Jn 2:2

4:15
John 6:69
1 Jn 5:5

4:17
1 Jn 2:5; 3:21

4:18
Rom 8:15

4:20
1 Jn 2:4; 3:17

4:21
Matt 5:43; 22:37-39

5:1
John 1:13; 3:3;
8:42

5:3
Matt 11:30
John 14:15

4:9 Jesus is God's *only* Son. While all believers are sons and daughters of God, only Jesus lives in this special unique relationship (see John 1:18; 3:16).

● **4:9, 10** Love explains: (1) why God creates—because he loves, he creates people to love; (2) why God cares—because he loves them, he cares for sinful people; (3) why we are free to choose—God wants a loving response from us; (4) why Christ died—his love for us caused him to offer a solution to the problem of sin; and (5) why we receive eternal life—God's love expresses itself to us forever.

4:10 Nothing sinful or evil can exist in God's presence. He is absolute goodness. He cannot overlook, condone, or excuse sin as though it never happened. He loves us, but his love does not make him morally lax. If we trust in Christ, however, we will not have to bear the penalty for our sins (1 Peter 2:24). We will be acquitted (Romans 5:18) by his atoning sacrifice.

● **4:12** If no one has ever seen God, how can we ever know him? John in his Gospel said, "The unique One, who is himself God, is near to the Father's heart. He has revealed God to us" (John 1:18). Jesus is the complete expression of God in human form, and he has revealed God to us. When we love one another, the invisible God reveals himself to others through us, and his love is made complete.

● **4:12** Some people simply enjoy being with others. They make friends with strangers easily and always are surrounded by friends. Other people are shy or reserved. They have a few friends and are frequently uncomfortable talking with people they don't know or mingling in crowds. Shy people don't need to become extroverts in order to love others. John isn't telling us *how many* people to love, but *how much* to love the people we already know. Our job is to love faithfully the people God has given us to love, whether there are two or two hundred of them. If God sees that we are ready to love others, he will bring them to us. No matter how shy we are, we don't need to be afraid of the love commandment. God provides us the strength to do what he asks.

● **4:13** When we become Christians, we receive the Holy Spirit. God's presence in our life is proof that we really belong to him. He also gives us the power to love (Romans 5:5; 8:9; 2 Corinthians 1:22). Rely on that power as you reach out to others. As you do so, you will gain confidence. See also Romans 8:16.

4:17 The day of judgment is that time when all people will appear before Christ and be held accountable for their actions. With God living in us through Christ, we have no reason to fear this day because we have been saved from punishment. Instead, we can look forward to the day of judgment because it will mean the end of sin and the beginning of a face-to-face relationship with Jesus Christ.

4:18 If we ever are afraid of the future, eternity, or God's judgment, we can remind ourselves of God's love. We know that he loves us perfectly (Romans 8:38, 39). We can resolve our fears first by focusing on his immeasurable love for us, and then by allowing him to love others through us. His love will quiet your fears and give you confidence.

● **4:19** God's love is the source of all human love, and it spreads like fire. In loving his children, God kindles a flame in their hearts. In turn, they love others, who are warmed by God's love through them.

● **4:20, 21** It is easy to say we love God when that love doesn't cost us anything more than weekly attendance at religious services. But the real test of our love for God is how we treat the people right in front of us—our family members and fellow believers. We cannot truly love God while neglecting to love those who are created in his image.

5:1, 2 When we become Christians, we become part of God's family, with fellow believers as our brothers and sisters. It is God who determines who the other family members are, not us. We are simply called to accept and love them. How well do you treat your fellow family members?

● **5:3, 4** Jesus never promised that obeying him would be easy. But the hard work and self-discipline of serving Christ is no

5:5
Rom 8:37

5:6
John 1:31-34; 14:7;
19:34-35

5:9
Matt 3:16-17
John 5:32-37;
8:17-18

5:10
John 3:33
Rom 8:16
Gal 4:6

5:12
John 3:15-16, 36;
5:24; 14:6; 17:2-3
2 Jn 1:9

and his commandments are not burdensome. ⁴For every child of God defeats this evil world, and we achieve this victory through our faith. ⁵And who can win this battle against the world? Only those who believe that Jesus is the Son of God.

⁶And Jesus Christ was revealed as God's Son by his baptism in water and by shedding his blood on the cross*—not by water only, but by water and blood. And the Spirit, who is truth, confirms it with his testimony. ⁷So we have these three witnesses*—⁸the Spirit, the water, and the blood—and all three agree. ⁹Since we believe human testimony, surely we can believe the greater testimony that comes from God. And God has testified about his Son. ¹⁰All who believe in the Son of God know in their hearts that this testimony is true. Those who don't believe this are actually calling God a liar because they don't believe what God has testified about his Son.

¹¹And this is what God has testified: He has given us eternal life, and this life is in his Son. ¹²Whoever has the Son has life; whoever does not have God's Son does not have life.

Conclusion

5:13
John 20:31

5:14
Matt 7:7
John 14:13; 15:7

5:16
Exod 23:21
Jer 7:16; 14:11
Matt 12:31
Heb 6:4-6; 10:26
Jas 5:15

5:18
John 10:28-29
1 Jn 2:13; 3:9

¹³I have written this to you who believe in the name of the Son of God, so that you may know you have eternal life. ¹⁴And we are confident that he hears us whenever we ask for anything that pleases him. ¹⁵And since we know he hears us when we make our requests, we also know that he will give us what we ask for.

¹⁶If you see a Christian brother or sister* sinning in a way that does not lead to death, you should pray, and God will give that person life. But there is a sin that leads to death, and I am not saying you should pray for those who commit it. ¹⁷All wicked actions are sin, but not every sin leads to death.

¹⁸We know that God's children do not make a practice of sinning, for God's Son holds them securely, and the evil one cannot touch them. ¹⁹We know that we are children of God and that the world around us is under the control of the evil one.

5:6 Greek *This is he who came by water and blood.* **5:7** A few very late manuscripts add *in heaven—the Father, the Word, and the Holy Spirit, and these three are one. And we have three witnesses on earth.* **5:16** Greek *a brother.*

---

burden to those who love him. And if our load starts to feel heavy, we can always trust Christ to help us bear it (see Matthew 11:28-30).

5:6-8 At this time, there was a false teaching in circulation that said Jesus was "the Christ" only between his baptism and his death—that is, he was merely human until he was baptized, at which time "the Christ" then descended upon him but then later left him before his death on the cross. But if Jesus died only as a man, he could not have taken upon himself the sins of the world, and Christianity would be an empty religion. Only an act of God could take away the punishment that we deserve for our sin.

5:7-9 The Gospels twice record God's clear declaration that Jesus was his Son—at Jesus' baptism (Matthew 3:16, 17) and at his transfiguration (Matthew 17:5).

5:12 Whoever believes in God's Son has eternal life. He is all you need. You don't need to *wait* for eternal life because it begins the moment you believe. You don't need to *work* for it because it is already yours. You don't need to *worry* about it because you have been given eternal life by God himself—and it is guaranteed.

5:13 Some people *hope* that they will receive eternal life. John says we can *know* we have it. Our certainty is based on God's promise that he has given us eternal life through his Son. This is true whether you feel close to God or far away from him. Eternal life is not based on feelings but on facts. You can know that you have eternal life if you believe God's truth. If you aren't sure that you are a Christian, ask yourself: Have I honestly committed my life to him as my Savior and Lord? If so, you know by faith that you are indeed a child of God.

• **5:14, 15** The emphasis here is on God's will, not our will. When we communicate with God, we don't demand what we want; rather we discuss with him what *he* wants for us. If we align our prayers to his will, he will listen; and we can be certain that if he listens, he will give us a definite answer. Start praying with confidence!

• **5:16, 17** Commentators differ widely in their thoughts about what this sin that leads to death is and whether the death it causes is physical or spiritual. Paul wrote that some Christians had died because they took Communion unworthily (1 Corinthians 11:27-30), and Ananias and Sapphira were struck dead when they lied to God (Acts 5:1-11). Blasphemy against the Holy Spirit results in spiritual death (Mark 3:29), and the book of Hebrews describes the spiritual death of the person who turns against Christ (Hebrews 6:4-6). John was probably referring to the people who had left the Christian fellowship and joined the antichrists. By rejecting the only way of salvation, these people were putting themselves out of reach of prayer. In most cases, however, even if we knew what the terrible sin was, we would have no sure way of knowing whether a certain person had committed it. Therefore, we should continue praying for our loved ones and for our Christian brothers and sisters, leaving the judgment up to God. Note that John says, "I am not saying you should pray for those who commit it," rather than, "You cannot pray for them." He recognized the lack of certainty.

• **5:18, 19** Christians commit sins, of course, but they ask God to forgive them, and then they continue serving him. God has freed believers from their slavery to Satan, and he keeps them safe from Satan's continued attacks. The rest of the world does not have the Christian's freedom to obey God. Unless they come to Christ in faith, they have no choice but to obey Satan. There is no middle ground; people either belong to God and obey him, or they live under Satan's control.

20And we know that the Son of God has come, and he has given us understanding so that we can know the true God.* And now we live in fellowship with the true God because we live in fellowship with his Son, Jesus Christ. He is the only true God, and he is eternal life.

21Dear children, keep away from anything that might take God's place in your hearts.*

5:20 Greek *the one who is true.*   **5:21** Greek *keep yourselves from idols.*

5:20
Luke 24:45
John 1:1, 4; 17:3
Rom 9:5
Rev 3:7

5:21
1 Cor 10:14
1 Thes 1:9

5:21 Many things can take God's place in our lives. This includes anything that substitutes for the true faith, anything that denies Christ's full deity and humanity, any human idea that claims to be more authoritative than the Bible, any loyalty that replaces God at the center of our life.

5:21 John presents a clear picture of Christ. What we think about Jesus Christ is central to our teaching, preaching, and living. Jesus is the God-man, fully God and fully human at the same time. He came to earth to die in our place for our sins. Through faith in him, we are given eternal life and the power to do his will. What is your answer to the most important question you could ever ask: Who is Jesus Christ?

2 JOHN

TRUTH and love are frequently discussed in our world but seldom practiced.

From politicians to marketers, people conveniently ignore or conceal facts and use words to enhance positions or sell products. Perjury is common, and integrity and credibility are endangered species. Words, twisted in meaning and torn from context, have become mere tools for ego building. It is not surprising that we have to "swear" to tell the truth.

And what about love? Our world is filled with its words: Popular songs, greeting cards, media counselors, and romantic novels shower us with notions and dreams of ethereal, idyllic relationships and feelings. Real love, however, is scarce—selfless giving, caring, sharing, and even dying. We yearn to love and be loved, but we see few living examples of real love. Plentiful are those who grasp, hoard, and watch out for "number one."

Christ is the antithesis of society's prevailing values, that is, falsehood and self-centeredness—for *he is truth and love* in person. Therefore, all who claim loyalty to him must be committed to these ideals—following the truth and living the truth, reflecting love and acting with love toward one another.

The apostle John had seen Truth and Love firsthand—he had been with Jesus. So affected was this disciple that all of his writings, from the Gospel to the book of Revelation, are filled with this theme: Truth and love are vital to the Christian and are inseparable in the Christian life. Second John, his brief letter to a dear friend, is no different. John says to live in the truth and obey God (1:4), watch out for deceivers (1:7), and love God and each other (1:6).

Second John will take just a few minutes to read, but its message should last a lifetime. As you reflect on these few paragraphs penned by the wise and aged follower of Christ, recommit yourself to being a person of truth, of love, and of obedience.

VITAL STATISTICS

PURPOSE:
To emphasize the basics of following Christ—truth and love—and to warn against false teachers

AUTHOR:
The apostle John

ORIGINAL AUDIENCE:
To "the chosen lady" and her children—or possibly to a local church

DATE WRITTEN:
About the same time as 1 John, approximately A.D. 90 from Ephesus

SETTING:
Evidently this woman and her family were involved in one of the churches that John was overseeing—they had developed a strong friendship with John. John was warning her of the false teachers who were becoming prevalent in some of the churches.

KEY VERSE:
"Love means doing what God has commanded us, and he has commanded us to love one another, just as you heard from the beginning " (1:6).

KEY PEOPLE:
John, the chosen lady, and her children

THE BLUEPRINT

1. Watch out for false teachers (1:1–11)
2. John's final words (1:12, 13)

False teachers were a dangerous problem for the church to which John was writing. His warning against showing hospitality to false teachers may sound harsh and unloving to many today. Yet these men were teaching heresy that could seriously harm many believers—for eternity.

MEGATHEMES

THEME	EXPLANATION	IMPORTANCE
Truth	Following God's Word, the Bible, is essential to Christian living because God is truth. Christ's true followers consistently obey his truth.	To be loyal to Christ's teaching, we must seek to know the Bible, but we may never twist its message to our own needs or purposes or encourage others who misuse it.
Love	Christ's command is for Christians to love one another. This is the basic ingredient of true Christianity.	To obey Christ fully, we must believe his command to love others. Helping, giving, and meeting needs put love into practice.
False Leaders	We must be wary of religious leaders who are not true to Christ's teaching. We should not give them a platform to spread false teaching.	Don't encourage those who are opposed to Christ. Politely remove yourself from association with false leaders. Be aware of what is being taught in your church.

1. Watch out for false teachers

Greetings

This letter is from John, the elder.*

I am writing to the chosen lady and to her children,* whom I love in the truth—as does everyone else who knows the truth—²because the truth lives in us and will be with us forever.

³Grace, mercy, and peace, which come from God the Father and from Jesus Christ—the Son of the Father—will continue to be with us who live in truth and love.

Live in the Truth

⁴How happy I was to meet some of your children and find them living according to the truth, just as the Father commanded.

⁵I am writing to remind you, dear friends,* that we should love one another. This is not a new commandment, but one we have had from the beginning. ⁶Love means doing what God has commanded us, and he has commanded us to love one another, just as you heard from the beginning.

⁷I say this because many deceivers have gone out into the world. They deny that Jesus

1:1
1 Pet 5:13
1 Jn 3:18-19
3 Jn 1:1
1:2
John 8:32; 14:17
1 Jn 1:8; 3:19
1:3
1 Tim 1:2
1:4
3 Jn 1:3-4
1:5
John 13:34; 15:12
1 Jn 2:7
1:6
John 14:15, 23-24
1 Jn 2:5, 7; 4:7-12;
5:3
1:7
1 Tim 4:1-5
2 Pet 2:1-3
1 Jn 2:18, 26; 4:1-3

1a Greek *From the elder.* **1b** Or *the church God has chosen and its members.* **5** Greek *I urge you, lady.*

1:1 The "elder" is John, one of Jesus' 12 disciples and the writer of the Gospel of John, three letters, and the book of Revelation. For more information about John, see his Profile in John 13, p. 1783. This letter was written shortly after 1 John to warn about false teachers. The salutation "to the chosen lady and to her children" could refer to a specific woman or to a church whose identity is no longer known. John may have written this from Ephesus.

1:1, 2 John wrote this second letter (which probably fit on one sheet of papyrus) to warn believers against inadvertently supporting false teachers. The number of itinerant evangelists and teachers had grown by the end of the first century; mixed in with the legitimate missionaries were others who were promoting heretical ideas about Christ and the gospel. Little has changed in two thousand years. Advocates of unorthodox beliefs still exist and still attempt to confuse and deceive the people of God. This letter, 2 John, should serve as a wake-up call to believers to be alert, to be careful, and to be solidly grounded in the faith. Are you prepared to recognize false doctrine?

• **1:3, 4** The "truth" is the truth about Jesus Christ, as opposed to the lies of the false teachers (see 1 John 2:21-23). John refers to truth five times in the first four verses of this brief letter. In contrast to so many in our culture who dogmatically deny truth ("There are no ultimate realities") or absurdly define it according to personal preference ("Your truth is your truth and my truth is my truth"), John declared the existence of an Absolute. God is that ultimate standard by which all else can be judged. God is true, his words and ways are true, and whatever or whoever contradicts or opposes him is false, deceptive,

and dangerous. Christian leaders, teachers, and parents must engage now in the difficult but critical battle for truth. To paraphrase a familiar saying: "All that is required for Deception to triumph is for the people of the Truth to do nothing." Begin an intentional campaign to teach those under your care how to distinguish between truth and error.

1:5, 6 The statement that Christians should love one another is a recurrent New Testament theme. Yet love for one's neighbor is an old command, first appearing in the third book of Moses (Leviticus 19:18). We can show love in many ways: by avoiding prejudice and discrimination; by accepting people; by listening, helping, giving, serving, and refusing to judge. Knowing God's command is not enough. We must put it into practice, "doing what God has commanded us" (see also Matthew 22:37-39 and 1 John 2:7, 8).

• **1:7** In John's day, many false teachers (deceivers) taught that spirit was good and matter was evil; therefore, they reasoned that Jesus could not have been both God and man. In strong terms, John warns against this kind of teaching. Many false teachers still promote an understanding of Jesus that is not biblical. These teachers are dangerous because they distort the truth and undermine the foundations of Christian faith. They may use the right words but change the meanings.

1:7 The term translated "deceivers" can also be translated "impostors"; it carries the idea of leading another astray. Notice that the verse refers to "many" such charlatans and pretenders. The great danger of deceitful leaders is that they seem so sincere and believable. They are not easy to spot in a crowd. Usually they are winsome and attractive; otherwise, how would they gather people to themselves? We do not want to become paranoid and

1:8
1 Cor 3:8-9

1:9
John 8:31
1 Jn 2:23

1:10
Rom 16:17
Eph 5:11

1:12
Num 12:8
1 Jn 1:4
3 Jn 1:13-14

Christ came* in a real body. Such a person is a deceiver and an antichrist. ⁸Watch out that you do not lose what we* have worked so hard to achieve. Be diligent so that you receive your full reward. ⁹Anyone who wanders away from this teaching has no relationship with God. But anyone who remains in the teaching of Christ has a relationship with both the Father and the Son.

¹⁰If anyone comes to your meeting and does not teach the truth about Christ, don't invite that person into your home or give any kind of encouragement. ¹¹Anyone who encourages such people becomes a partner in their evil work.

2. John's final words

¹²I have much more to say to you, but I don't want to do it with paper and ink. For I hope to visit you soon and talk with you face to face. Then our joy will be complete.

¹³Greetings from the children of your sister,* chosen by God.

7 Or *will come.* **8** Some manuscripts read *you.* **13** Or *from the members of your sister church.*

---

suspicious about everyone we meet, but we do need to be wise in evaluating the character and conduct of those who would seek to influence people. The way your teachers live shows a lot about what they believe about Christ. For more on testing teachers, see 1 John 4:1.

• **1:8** To "receive your full reward" refers not to salvation but to the rewards of loyal service. All who value the truth and persistently hold to it will win their full reward. Those who live for themselves and justify their self-centeredness by teaching false doctrines will lose that reward (see Matthew 7:21-23).

• **1:10** John instructs the believers not to show hospitality to false teachers. They were to do nothing that would encourage the heretics in their propagation of falsehoods. In addition, if believers were to invite them in, such action would show that they were approving of what the false teachers said and did. John is condemning the support of those who are dedicated to opposing the true teachings of God, not condemning hospitality to unbelievers. John adds that a person who supports a false teacher in any way shares in the teacher's evil work.

• **1:10** False teaching is serious business, and we dare not overlook it. It is so serious that John wrote this letter to warn against it. Because our world has so many false teachings, we might be tempted to take many of them lightly. Instead, we should realize the dangers they pose and actively refuse to give heresies any foothold.

3 JOHN

VITAL STATISTICS

PURPOSE:
To commend Gaius for his hospitality and to encourage him in his Christian life

AUTHOR:
The apostle John

ORIGINAL AUDIENCE:
Gaius, a prominent Christian in one of the churches known to John

DATE WRITTEN:
Approximately A.D. 90 from Ephesus

SETTING:
Church leaders traveled from town to town helping to establish new congregations. They depended on the hospitality of fellow believers. Gaius was one who welcomed these leaders into his home.

KEY VERSE:
"Dear friend, you are being faithful to God when you care for the traveling teachers who pass through, even though they are strangers to you" (1:5).

KEY PEOPLE:
John, Gaius, Diotrephes, Demetrius

BY SPECIAL invitation or with a surprise knock, company arrives and with them comes the promise of soiled floors, extra laundry, dirty dishes, altered schedules, personal expense, and inconvenience. From sharing a meal to providing a bed, *hospitality* costs . . . in time, energy, and money. But how we treat others reflects our true values—what is really important to us. Do we see people as objects or inconveniences, or as unique creations of a loving God? And which is more important to God, a person or a carpet? Perhaps the most effective way to demonstrate God's values and Christ's love to others is to invite and welcome guests into our homes.

For Gaius, hospitality was a habit, and his reputation for friendship and generosity, especially to traveling teachers and missionaries (1:5), had spread. To affirm and thank Gaius for his Christian lifestyle, and to encourage him in his faith, John wrote this personal note.

John's format for this letter centers around three men: Gaius, the example of one who follows Christ and loves others (1:1–8); Diotrephes, the self-proclaimed church leader who does not reflect God's values (1:9–11); and Demetrius, who also follows the truth (1:12). John encourages Gaius to practice hospitality, continue to walk in the truth, and do what is right.

Although this is a personal letter, we can look over the shoulder of Gaius and apply its lessons to our life. As you read 3 John, with which man do you identify? Are you a Gaius, generously giving to others? a Demetrius, loving the truth? or a Diotrephes, looking out for yourself and your things? Determine to reflect Christ's values in your relationships, opening your home and touching others with his love.

THE BLUEPRINT

1. God's children live by the standards of the gospel
(1:1–12)
2. John's final words
(1:13–15)

John wrote to commend Gaius, who was taking care of traveling teachers and missionaries, and to warn against people like Diotrephes, who was proud and refused to listen to spiritual leaders in authority. If we are to live in the truth of the gospel, we must look for ways to support pastors, Christian workers, and missionaries today. All Christians should work together to support God's work both at home and around the world.

MEGATHEMES

THEME	EXPLANATION	IMPORTANCE
Hospitality	John wrote to encourage those who were kind to others. Genuine hospitality for traveling Christian workers was needed then and is still important today.	Faithful Christian teachers and missionaries need our support. Whenever you can extend hospitality to others, it will make you a partner in their ministry.
Pride	Diotrephes not only refused to offer hospitality but also set himself up as a church boss. Pride disqualified him from being a real leader.	Christian leaders must shun pride and its effects on them. Be careful not to misuse your position of leadership.
Faithfulness	Gaius and Demetrius were commended for their faithful work in the church. They were held up as examples of faithful, selfless servants.	Don't take for granted Christian workers who serve faithfully. Be sure to encourage them so they won't grow weary of serving.

1. God's children live by the standards of the gospel

1:1
2 Jn 1:1

Greetings

This letter is from John, the elder.*

1:3
2 Jn 1:4

I am writing to Gaius, my dear friend, whom I love in the truth.

1:4
1 Cor 4:15
Gal 4:19
1 Jn 2:1

²Dear friend, I hope all is well with you and that you are as healthy in body as you are strong in spirit. ³Some of the traveling teachers* recently returned and made me very happy by telling me about your faithfulness and that you are living according to the truth. ⁴I could have no greater joy than to hear that my children are following the truth.

1:5
Rom 12:13
Heb 13:2
1 Pet 4:10

Caring for the Lord's Workers

1:6
Col 1:10
Titus 3:13

⁵Dear friend, you are being faithful to God when you care for the traveling teachers who pass through, even though they are strangers to you. ⁶They have told the church here of your loving friendship. Please continue providing for such teachers in a manner that pleases God. ⁷For they are traveling for the Lord,* and they accept nothing from people who are not

1:7
Matt 10:9-14
Mark 6:8-13
Luke 9:3-5; 10:4-11
Acts 20:33, 35

1 Greek *From the elder.*   3 Greek *the brothers;* also in verses 5 and 10.   7a Greek *They went out on behalf of the Name.*

●**1:1** This letter provides us an important glimpse into the life of the early church. Third John, addressed to Gaius, highlights the need for showing hospitality to traveling preachers and other believers. It also warns against a would-be church dictator.

●**1:1** The "elder," John, was one of Jesus' 12 disciples and the writer of the Gospel of John, three letters, and the book of Revelation. For more information about John, see his Profile in John 13, p. 1783. We have no further information about Gaius, but he is someone whom John loved dearly. Perhaps Gaius had shared his home and hospitality with John at some time during John's travels. If so, John would have appreciated his actions because traveling preachers depended on expressions of hospitality to survive (see Matthew 10:11-16).

1:2 John was concerned for Gaius's physical *and* spiritual well-being. This was the opposite of the popular heresy that taught the separation of spirit and matter and despised the physical side of life. Today, many people still fall into this way of thinking. This non-Christian attitude logically leads to one of two responses: neglect of the body and physical health, or indulgence of the body's sinful desires. God is concerned for both your body and your soul. As a responsible Christian, you should neither neglect nor indulge yourself but care for your physical needs and discipline your body so that you are at your best for God's service.

1:4 John writes about "my children" because, as a result of his preaching, he was the spiritual father of many, including Gaius.

●**1:5, 6** In the church's early days, traveling prophets, evangelists, and teachers were helped on their way by people like Gaius, who housed and fed them. Hospitality is a lost art in many churches today. We would do well to invite more people for meals—fellow church members, young people, traveling missionaries, those in need, visitors. This is an active and much-appreciated way to show your love. In fact, it is probably more important today. Because of our individualistic, self-centered society, many lonely people wonder if anyone cares whether they live or die. If you find such a lonely person, show him or her that *you* care!

●**1:7** The traveling missionaries neither asked for nor accepted anything from nonbelievers. This was not intended to be a criticism of unbelievers, but a statement of how things ought to be. Imagine the awkwardness of a Christian worker's requesting funds or lodging from the very people he or she was trying to reach! Instead, it is the responsibility of churches and Christian individuals to support those who are called by God to full-time vocational ministry. In that way, unbelievers will not be questioning the missionaries' motives for preaching. God's true preachers do not preach to make money but to fulfill their calling and express their love for God. It is the church's responsibility to care for Christian workers; this should never be left to nonbelievers. Don't just automatically discard the next missionary fund-raising letter you receive. That appeal may be God's invitation for you to become a partner in a new gospel venture.

believers.* ⁸So we ourselves should support them so that we can be their partners as they teach the truth.

⁹I wrote to the church about this, but Diotrephes, who loves to be the leader, refuses to have anything to do with us. ¹⁰When I come, I will report some of the things he is doing and the evil accusations he is making against us. Not only does he refuse to welcome the traveling teachers, he also tells others not to help them. And when they do help, he puts them out of the church.

1:10
John 9:22, 34
2 Jn 1:12
3 Jn 1:5

¹¹Dear friend, don't let this bad example influence you. Follow only what is good. Remember that those who do good prove that they are God's children, and those who do evil prove that they do not know God.*

1:11
Ps 34:14
1 Jn 2:29; 3:6, 9-10

¹²Everyone speaks highly of Demetrius, as does the truth itself. We ourselves can say the same for him, and you know we speak the truth.

1:12
John 19:35; 21:24

2. John's final words

¹³I have much more to say to you, but I don't want to write it with pen and ink. ¹⁴For I hope to see you soon, and then we will talk face to face.

1:13
Num 12:8
2 Jn 1:12

¹⁵*Peace be with you.

Your friends here send you their greetings. Please give my personal greetings to each of our friends there.

1:14
2 Jn 1:12

7b Greek *from Gentiles.*   **11** Greek *they have not seen God.*   **15** Some English translations combine verses 14 and 15 into verse 14.

• **1:8** When you help someone who is spreading the Good News, you are in a very real way a partner in the ministry. This is the other side of the principle in 2 John 1:10 (see the note there). Not everyone should go to the mission field; those who work for Christ at home are vital to the ministry of those who go and who need support. We can support missionaries by praying for them and by giving our money, hospitality, and time.

1:9 This letter to which John refers was neither 1 nor 2 John but another letter that no longer exists.

• **1:9, 10** All we know about Diotrephes is that he wanted to control the church. John denounced: (1) his refusal to have anything to do with other spiritual leaders, (2) his slander of the leaders, (3) his bad example in refusing to welcome any teachers, and (4) his attempt to excommunicate those who opposed his leadership. Sins such as pride, jealousy, and slander are still present in the church, and when a leader makes a habit of encouraging sin and discouraging right actions, he or she must be stopped. If no one speaks up, great harm can come to the church. We must confront sin in the church; if we ignore it, it will continue to grow. A true Christian leader is a servant, not an autocrat!

• **1:12** We know nothing about Demetrius except that he may have carried this letter from John to Gaius. The book of Acts mentions an Ephesian silversmith named Demetrius, who opposed Paul (Acts 19:24ff), but this is probably another man. In contrast to the corrupt Diotrephes, Demetrius had a high regard for truth. John personified truth as a witness to Demetrius's character and teaching. In other words, if truth could speak, it would speak on Demetrius's behalf. When Demetrius arrived, Gaius certainly opened his home to him.

• **1:14** Whereas 2 John emphasizes the need to refuse hospitality to false teachers, 3 John urges continued hospitality to those who teach the truth. Hospitality is a strong sign of support for people and their work. It means giving of your resources to them so their stay will be comfortable and their work and travel easier. Actively look for creative ways to show hospitality to God's workers. It may be in the form of a letter of encouragement, a gift, financial support, an open home, or prayer.

STUDY QUESTIONS

Thirteen lessons for individual or group study

It's always exciting to get more than you expect. And that's what you'll find in this Bible study guide—much more than you expect. Our goal was to write thoughtful, practical, dependable, and application-oriented studies of God's word.

This study guide contains the complete text of the selected Bible book. The commentary is accurate, complete, and loaded with unique charts, maps, and profiles of Bible people.

With the Bible text, extensive notes and features, and questions to guide discussion, Life Application Bible Studies have everything you need in one place.

The lessons in this Bible-study guide will work for large classes as well as small-group studies. To get everyone involved in your discussions, encourage participants to answer the questions before each meeting.

Each lesson is divided into five easy-to-lead sections. The section called "Reflect" introduces you and the members of your group to a specific area of life touched by the lesson. "Read" shows which chapters to read and which notes and other features to use. Additional questions help you understand the passage. "Realize" brings into focus the biblical principle to be learned with questions, a special insight, or both. "Respond" helps you make connections with your own situation and personal needs. The questions are designed to help you find areas in your life where you can apply the biblical truths. "Resolve" helps you map out action plans for that day.

Begin and end each lesson with prayer, asking for the Holy Spirit's guidance, direction, and wisdom.

Recommended time allotments for each section of a lesson are as follows:

Segment	60 minutes	90 minutes
Reflect on your life	*5 minutes*	*10 minutes*
Read the passage	*10 minutes*	*15 minutes*
Realize the principle	*15 minutes*	*20 minutes*
Respond to the message	*20 minutes*	*30 minutes*
Resolve to take action	*10 minutes*	*15 minutes*

All five sections work together to help a person learn the lessons, live out the principles, and obey the commands taught in the Bible.

Also, at the end of each lesson, there is a section entitled "More for studying other themes in this section." These questions will help you lead the group in studying other parts of each section not covered in depth by the main lesson.

But don't just listen to God's word. You must do what it says. Otherwise, you are only fooling yourselves. For if you listen to the word and don't obey, it is like glancing at your face in a mirror. You see yourself, walk away, and forget what you look like. But if you look carefully into the perfect law that sets you free, and if you do what it says and don't forget what you heard, then God will bless you for doing it (James 1:22-25).

LESSON 1
EYEWITNESS!
1 JOHN 1:1-4

REFLECT
on your life

1 How have you heard the word *eyewitness* used this past week?

_____

_____

_____

2 What makes eyewitness testimony so convincing in a court of law?

_____

_____

_____

_____

READ
the passage

Read the introduction to 1 John, 1 John 1:1-4, and the following notes:

❏ 1:1   ❏ 1:1-5   ❏ 1:3

3 Why was John qualified to write this letter about having confidence in the faith?

_____

_____

_____

4 Briefly describe what happened to the apostles and the Christian church—between Jesus' ascension and the writing of this letter—that caused some Christians to doubt their faith.

_____

_____

_____

5 Why were some Christians having doubts about their faith?

_____

_____

_____

6 What were these early Christians doubting?

_____

_____

_____

Eyewitness testimony carries a lot of weight with people. When an interesting event takes place, reporters look for eyewitnesses to interview. In a court of law, verdicts can hinge on the testimony of a star witness. It is no wonder that God used eyewitnesses to convey the truth about his Son, Jesus. John was one such eyewitness. He had heard, seen, and touched Jesus—the Word of life. And he recorded what he had seen and heard. Why? To reassure believers who had not seen Jesus that their faith was justified. John wanted their fellowship with God not to be hindered by doubt. We haven't seen Jesus, but we can know the facts about him. We can rely on John's eyewitness account.

REALIZE
the principle

7 What doubts do some Christians have about their faith?

_____

_____

_____

8 What causes their doubts?

_____

_____

_____

_____

9 How can God's Word in 1 John help them overcome their doubts?

_____

_____

_____

_____

10 What doubts have you had about your faith?

RESPOND
to the message

_____

_____

_____

_____

11 How do the words of an eyewitness to Jesus' ministry help you deal with your doubts?

_____

_____

_____

_____

12 John was also an eyewitness to the events following the birth of the church— the answered prayers, the severe persecution, and the faith of the new Christians. He himself endured persecution. What does John's proclamation of eternal life (1:2) mean to you in light of his experience?

_____

_____

_____

_____

13 What truths about the faith are important to you?

RESOLVE
to take action

_____

_____

_____

_____

14 How can you reaffirm your confidence in these truths this week?

_____

_____

_____

_____

A What does it mean that Jesus is the "Word of life" (1:1)? How has Jesus changed your life so far?

B John wrote so that his readers would "have fellowship" with him, with other Christians, and with God (1:3). How is Christian fellowship different from merely spending time with people? If John's goal is being achieved in your life, what does this fellowship mean in your day-to-day experience?

MORE
for studying
other themes
in this section

LESSON 2
IN THE LIGHT
1 JOHN 1:5–2:2

REFLECT
on your life

1 Describe a time when you were dirty from head to toe.

_____

_____

_____

_____

_____

2 What did it take to get clean?

_____

_____

_____

_____

READ
the passage

Read 1 John 1:5–2:2 and the following notes:

❏ 1:5, 6   ❏ 1:6   ❏ 1:7   ❏ 1:8   ❏ 1:8-10   ❏ 1:9   ❏ 2:1, 2   ❏ 2:2

3 Why can no one claim to be without sin (1:8, 10)? Why is it impossible for Christians to live without sinning?

_____

_____

_____

4 What provision has God made for us to deal with our sin (1:9)?

_____

_____

5 How does he provide forgiveness (2:1-2)? Why?

_____

_____

_____

John's audience had been hearing many false teachings about sin. Some false teachers said that sin didn't affect a person's relationship with God at all. Some said that the sinful nature was dead and people could become completely sinless. Others denied the existence of sin altogether. John began his letter by attacking all those ideas. Sin is real, and all people sin. God does distinguish between those who persistently sin and those who don't (1:6-7). The bottom line is: All Christians must deal with sin. If we were capable of living without sin, then Jesus would not have needed to die as the sacrifice for our sins and for the sins of all the world (2:2). We would not need confession, and we would not need Christ. In reality, all of us are guilty before God and need to be purified from sin. Fortunately, God has made a way. If we confess our sins, God is _faithful_ and _just_ and will _forgive_ us and _cleanse_ us (1:9).

REALIZE
the principle

6 How does sin make us dirty or impure?

_____

_____

_____

7 What happens when we confess our sins (1:9)?

_____

_____

_____

8 How does confession make us clean or pure?

_____

_____

_____

9 Why do we need to confess our sins if Christ has already paid for them with his blood?

_____

_____

_____

10 What is the difference between a person who lives "in the light" and one who lives "in spiritual darkness"?

_____

_____

_____

11 How often do we need to confess our sins?

_____

_____

_____

RESPOND
to the message

12 What is the process for confessing our sins?

_____

_____

_____

13 How does regular confession help you live "in the light"?

_____

_____

_____

_____

14 What do you need to do to make confession a regular part of your life?

_____

_____

_____

RESOLVE
to take action

15 What do you need to do to live "in the light"?

_____

_____

_____

_____

16 What will you confess to God right now?

_____

_____

_____

A What does it mean that "God is light" (1:5)?

B How does Jesus' blood cleanse us from every sin (1:7)? What must we do in order for Jesus to cleanse us?

C What hope is there for a person who sins (2:1)? How can you benefit from this hope?

D What is Jesus doing right now for us (2:1)? How does that truth affect the way you live?

MORE
for studying
other themes
in this section

LESSON 3
SOMETHING OLD, SOMETHING NEW
1 JOHN 2:3-14

REFLECT
on your life

1 What kind of people do you like to be around?

_____

_____

_____

_____

2 How can you tell when people like you?

_____

_____

_____

READ
the passage

Read 1 John 2:3-14 and the following notes:

❒ 2:3-6 ❒ 2:6 ❒ 2:7, 8 ❒ 2:9-11

3 What undeniable fact is revealed by Christians who live as Jesus did (2:3-6)?

_____

_____

_____

4 If the command to love is old, how is it also new (2:7, 8)?

_____

_____

_____

5 What is the evidence that a person is wandering in spiritual darkness (2:11)?

_____

_____

_____

John wrote, in no uncertain terms, that if we claim to know and love God, we must show this by doing what God commands. Otherwise, we really don't know him. For example, we cannot claim to love God and hate a brother. And who are our brothers? Fellow believers—members of the family of God. The way we treat others is the measure of our love and obedience. We can be assured that we belong to Christ if our faith shows itself in loving actions toward our brothers and sisters.

REALIZE
the principle

6 List some objections to the principle that the way we treat others is the measure of our obedience to God.

_____

_____

_____

_____

_____

7 Why do believers have to be told to love others?

_____

_____

_____

8 What are some of the barriers to loving others?

_____

_____

_____

_____

9 What kind of love did John intend for us to have?

_____

_____

_____

RESPOND
to the message

10 What kind of people are easy for you to love?

_____

_____

_____

11 What kind of people are difficult for you to love?

_____

_____

_____

12 What loving actions have you seen in your church?

_____

_____

_____

13 List some ways that you can show love to others:

_____

_____

_____

_____

14 How can you show love to people whom you don't really like?

_____

_____

_____

_____

RESOLVE
to take action

15 Think of someone you've treated unkindly or from whom you've simply with-held a kindness. What can you do to show love toward this person?

_____

_____

_____

_____

A What does it mean that "the true light is already shining" (2:8)?

B Explain John's repetition of "I am writing to you" and "I have written to you" in 2:12-14. What is his point in these verses?

MORE
for studying
other themes
in this section

LESSON 4
WORLDLY WISE
1 JOHN 2:15-17

REFLECT
on your life

1 Think of a current TV advertisement for an automobile. To what human desires does it appeal?

_____

_____

_____

_____

_____

2 What message is the ad trying to give in order to get you to buy the car?

_____

_____

_____

_____

_____

READ
the passage

Read 1 John 2:15-17 and the following notes:

❏ 2:15, 16   ❏ 2:17

3 What is wrong with loving the world (2:15-17)?

_____

_____

_____

_____

4 Give examples from 1 John 2:16 of . . .

"a craving for physical pleasure"

_____

_____

_____

"a craving for everything we see"

_____

_____

_____

"pride in our achievements and possessions"

_____

_____

_____

Living only for this life can be attractive and tempting and even an obsession if we are not careful. Sex and other physical desires, wealth and material possessions, power and pride—all demand our devotion and loyalty. These attractions will pass away and pull us away from God. In contrast, God and doing his will last forever. God wants first place in our life. How much better to focus on what pleases God and has eternal significance than to waste our life "chasing the wind" (Ecclesiastes 1:14).

REALIZE
the principle

5 How do God's values clash with the world's values?

_____

_____

_____

_____

6 How can a person keep the love of God foremost in his or her life?

_____

_____

_____

RESPOND
to the message

7 What sinful cravings are many people preoccupied with satisfying?

_____

_____

_____

_____

_____

8 What lusts tempt our eyes today?

_____

_____

_____

_____

_____

9 How do people work to elevate their status or standing?

_____

_____

_____

_____

_____

10 Which of these areas of "the world" is most tempting to you?

_____

_____

_____

_____

_____

11 What areas of your life are most affected when you love God and do his will instead of loving the world?

_____

_____

_____

_____

12 What can you do to keep God, not the enticements of the world, as the focus of your life?

RESOLVE
to take action

_____

_____

_____

_____

_____

_____

A How can we enjoy life and the blessings God gives us and yet follow the command not to love the world?

B Describe some current advertisements designed to whet our physical cravings for pleasure, possessions, or achievements. How can we serve as advertisements to others to whet their spiritual appetites?

MORE
for studying
other themes
in this section

LESSON 5
IT'S THE TRUTH
1 JOHN 2:18-27

REFLECT
on your life

1 How can you tell when someone is lying to you?

_____

_____

_____

_____

_____

READ
the passage

Read 1 John 2:18-27 and the following notes:

❐ 2:18-23 ❐ 2:19 ❐ 2:20 ❐ 2:22, 23 ❐ 2:24 ❐ 2:26, 27

2 John warned that Christians must always be wary of "antichrists" (2:18-27).

Who were they?

_____

_____

Where did they come from?

_____

_____

What were they teaching?

_____

_____

What kind of people are led astray by these false teachers?

_____

_____

3 How can believers identify antichrists (2:22)?

_____

_____

_____

_____

4 How can believers avoid being led astray (2:23-25)?

_____

_____

_____

_____

When John wrote his letter, some people were teaching false doctrines and trying to draw weak Christians away from Christ. So John wrote to reassure the young believers of their faith. "Antichrists," false Christians, were claiming faith in God while denying that Christ was God's Son. John warned against such antichrists and reassured the Christians that they could stand firm in their faith and not be lured away from the truth. False teachers peddle their ideas today as well. Their variations on orthodoxy may sound good, but the true test of their authenticity is: What do they say about Christ? We must reject any teacher, whether in the church or not, who denies the deity of Christ.

REALIZE
the principle

5 What basic teachings about Christ must a Christian affirm or believe?

_____

_____

_____

_____

6 Why is it important for Christians to review the basics of the Christian faith?

_____

_____

_____

R
RESPOND
to the message

7 What false teachings about Christ have you heard recently?

_____

_____

_____

_____

_____

8 Why are people attracted to false teachings?

_____

_____

_____

_____

9 What false teachings about Christ are some Christians tempted to believe?

_____

_____

_____

_____

_____

10 To avoid being led astray by an antichrist, you must know the truth well. What resources might help you know the truth better?

_____

_____

_____

_____

11 How can you test various teachings against the truth? What questions should you ask?

_____

_____

_____

_____

_____

12 Whom do you know who seems to be interested in a false teaching or cult?

_____

_____

_____

_____

13 What will you do to reassure that person of the truth about Christ?

_____

_____

_____

_____

_____

A When is "the last hour" (2:18)? How do we know? How should knowing that we are living in the last hour affect the way we live?

B What is the significance of John's words that the antichrists came from the church (2:19)? Where and when have you seen this happen? What have you learned from it?

C What does "the Holy One has given you his Spirit" mean (2:20-27)? How can you rely upon him when dealing with antichrists?

MORE
for studying
other themes
in this section

LESSON 6
IT'S ALL IN THE ATTITUDE
1 JOHN 2:28–3:10

REFLECT
on your life

1 List some typical bad habits of others that really bother you.

_____

_____

_____

_____

2 What makes habits so difficult to break?

_____

_____

_____

_____

_____

READ
the passage

Read 1 John 2:28–3:10 and the following notes:

❒ 2:28, 29   ❒ 3:2, 3   ❒ 3:4ff   ❒ 3:5   ❒ 3:8, 9   ❒ 3:9

3 How can God's children be "full of courage and not shrink back . . . in shame" when Christ returns (2:28)?

_____

_____

_____

_____

4 What does the future hold for God's children (2:28; 3:2)?

_____

_____

_____

5 Since Christians know that Christ is returning, how should they conduct themselves (3:3)?

_____

_____

_____

6 Who are the children of God and the children of the devil (3:7-10)?

_____

_____

_____

God has promised a great future to his children. John reassured these believers that they would participate in that future if they would continue to do what is right. One test of a person's faith is his or her attitude toward sin. Even Christians sin, but there is a difference between *sinning* and *continuing to sin.* The genuine believer in Christ recognizes sin for the evil that it is and fights it, whereas the person who continues to sin makes no real effort to respond to God's moral law. If we do what is right and refuse to keep on sinning, and if we truly love others, we can be confident that we are God's children and will be able to stand unashamed before him at his return.

REALIZE
the principle

7 All people sin. How then does the life of a conscientious Christian differ from that of an unbeliever?

_____

_____

_____

_____

8 How is it possible for a person to be sinful and yet do what is right?

_____

_____

_____

9 What sometimes shakes your confidence in your identity as a child of God?

_____

_____

_____

_____

_____

10 What evidence of struggle against sin is there in your . . .

prayer life? _____

_____

interactions with family? _____

_____

work habits? _____

_____

use of free time? _____

_____

11 John wrote that doing what is right can give us courage when Christ returns (2:28). What adjustments can you make in your life to become more courageous and unashamed to meet Christ?

_____

_____

_____

_____

_____

_____

12 What truth(s) from this passage do you want to remember throughout this week?

_____

_____

_____

_____

A What will happen to Christians when Christ appears (3:2)? In what ways is this already happening in your life? How should this knowledge affect the way you live?

MORE
for studying
other themes
in this section

B What did Jesus do to destroy the devil's work (3:8)? How does this affect you?

C How can you know who is a true child of God (3:10)? What evidence is there in your life that you are in God's family?

LESSON 7
TRUE LOVE
1 JOHN 3:11-24

REFLECT
on your life

1 When have you heard the word *love* used in the last two days?

_____

_____

_____

_____

2 Describe a loving act that someone has done for you.

_____

_____

_____

_____

_____

_____

READ
the passage

Read 1 John 3:11-24 and the following notes:

❏ 3:15   ❏ 3:16   ❏ 3:17, 18   ❏ 3:19, 20   ❏ 3:23   ❏ 3:24

3 Trace the phrase "we know," "you know," and "he [God] knows" throughout this passage (3:11-24). Write out what is known.

You know (3:15)

_____

_____

We know (3:16)

_____

_____

God knows (3:20)

_____

_____

We know (3:24)

_____

_____

4 What is the evidence that God's love is in us (3:17)?

_____

_____

_____

_____

5 What does real love involve (3:18)?

_____

_____

_____

_____

At this point in his letter John returned to the topic of love—specifically, love for other Christians. By our love for others, we know that we belong to God. And what is love? Jesus gave us the standard—serving others. It's easy to talk about love and to say we love certain people. But the true test of love is how we act toward them. If we truly love others, we will act like we love them, working hard to meet their needs, to serve them, and to help them—even at our own expense.

REALIZE
the principle

6 Why is love so important?

_____

_____

_____

7 Most people would never murder someone, so why did John use the example of Cain (3:12) and tell us not to be like him?

_____

_____

_____

8 What is the difference between "say[ing] . . . we love each other" and loving "by our actions" (3:18)?

_____

_____

_____

_____

_____

RESPOND
to the message

9 In what practical ways can we "give up our lives for our brothers and sisters" (3:16)?

_____

_____

_____

_____

10 How can we use our money to help others?

_____

_____

_____

_____

_____

11 What worldly goods do you have that you could use to help others in need?

_____

_____

_____

_____

12 Write down the name of at least one person whom you want to make a special effort to love in action and truth.

RESOLVE
to take action

_____

13 What can you do this week for this person?

_____

_____

_____

_____

_____

MORE
for studying
other themes
in this section

A How does the world show its hate for those who believe in God and in Christ (3:13)? How have you been persecuted for your faith? How should Christians respond to opposition?

B Why might we feel guilty (3:20, 21)? What reassurance do we have should that happen (3:19-22)? What does it mean to you that "God is greater than our feelings, and he knows everything"?

C In what sense can we receive anything we request from God (3:22)? How should this truth affect your prayer life?

D How do we know that God lives in us (3:24)? How do other people know that God lives in you?

LESSON 8
CHEAP IMITATIONS
1 JOHN 4:1-6

REFLECT
on your life

1 What product imitations have you purchased in the past?

_____

_____

_____

_____

2 Describe a time when you were disappointed with an imitation. Why were you disappointed?

_____

_____

_____

_____

_____

_____

READ
the passage

Read 1 John 4:1-6, the "Heresies" article, and the following notes:

❏ 4:1, 2   ❏ 4:6

3 What imitations did John warn Christians about (4:1-3)?

_____

_____

_____

4 What can Christians do about false prophets (4:1-3)?

_____

_____

_____

5 Describe the false teachings that were popular in John's day and why they were popular (see the "Heresies" article):

Docetism

_____

_____

_____

_____

Gnosticism

_____

_____

_____

_____

There were many false prophets in the early days of the church. They had their own agenda and wanted to support their position, but they did not necessarily want to submit to Christ as Savior and Lord. John told his readers to test these prophets and to reject any who did not pass the test. John reassured them that they had what was needed to tell the difference between true and false prophets.

REALIZE
the principle

There are many false prophets in the world today, too—men and women who falsely claim to speak for God. Sometimes their messages sound appealing or true. In order not to be fooled, Christians can use this test: Do these people believe that Jesus is God and man? To deny either aspect of Christ's nature is to deny Christ.

6 Why do some people have difficulty believing that Jesus was both divine and human?

_____

_____

_____

_____

7 How have Christians already won their fight with false prophets (4:4)?

_____

_____

_____

8 What are some imitations of Christianity today?

_____

_____

_____

_____

_____

9 How do you know the imitations of Christianity are not true?

_____

_____

_____

_____

RESPOND
to the message

10 How can Christians test a "prophet" to find out if he or she is teaching true Christian doctrine?

_____

_____

_____

_____

_____

11 What have you heard lately that sounds like a false version of Christianity (or a false doctrine)?

_____

_____

_____

_____

_____

12 How can a Christian respond to someone who is teaching false ideas about Christ?

_____

_____

_____

_____

13 As you talk to friends or read books and magazines, what can you do to "test the spirits"?

RESOLVE
to take action

_____

_____

_____

_____

_____

A Who is "the spirit who lives in the world" (4:4)? Who is "the Spirit who lives in you" (4:4)? What difference does it make that "the Spirit who lives in you is greater than the spirit who lives in the world" (4:4)?

MORE
for studying
other themes
in this section

B When have you been rejected for your belief in Christ? How can that experience strengthen your faith?

LESSON 9
THE MEANING OF SACRIFICE
1 JOHN 4:7-21

REFLECT
on your life

1 How did your parents sacrifice for you when you were young?

_____

_____

_____

_____

_____

READ
the passage

Read 1 John 4:7-21 and the following notes:

❐ 4:7ff   ❐ 4:8   ❐ 4:9, 10   ❐ 4:12   ❐ 4:13   ❐ 4:19   ❐ 4:20, 21

2 As you read this section (4:7-21), count the number of times the word _love_ is used. Then write a definition of love from what you read in the passage.

_____

_____

_____

_____

_____

3 How did God show his love for us (4:9-10)?

_____

_____

_____

_____

4 Why is it essential for Christians to love one another (4:20)?

_____

_____

_____

_____

_____

Returning to the theme of love, John now focuses our attention on the source of love, God, and what God's love cost. God showed his love by sending his Son to die for us. The miracle is that God loved us while we were sinners, and that Christ sacrificed his very life for us. This shows us what God's kind of love is—a willingness to sacrifice for someone else. God loved us by giving until it hurt. That is the kind of love he asks us to have for one another.

REALIZE
the principle

5 What are the differences between the world's idea of love and God's love?

_____

_____

_____

_____

_____

6 Which of God's actions demonstrate his love?

_____

_____

_____

_____

_____

7 How does God use Christians to show his love to the world?

_____

_____

_____

_____

_____

RESPOND
to the message

8 When and where is it especially difficult for you to love others?

_____

_____

_____

_____

_____

9 What sacrifices might it take for you to love as Christ loved in the situation(s) you described above?

_____

_____

_____

_____

_____

RESOLVE
to take action

10 What sacrifices will you make this week to demonstrate love to the difficult people in your life?

_____

_____

_____

_____

_____

_____

MORE
for studying
other themes
in this section

A What has Jesus done for you (4:10)? What can you do for him?

B What does it mean that . . .

God is life (1:1, 2)?

God is light (1:5)?

God is love (4:16)?

LESSON 10
WE CAN OVERCOME
1 JOHN 5:1-12

REFLECT
on your life

1 Think of someone you know or know about who has overcome a habit or tragedy because of his or her faith in God. What did that person overcome?

_____

_____

_____

_____

_____

2 What impressed you most about how that person overcame this difficulty?

_____

_____

_____

_____

_____

READ
the passage

Read 1 John 5:1-12 and the following note:

❏ 5:3, 4

3 What does it mean that God's commands are not burdensome (5:3-4)?

_____

_____

_____

_____

_____

4 How can Christians defeat "this evil world" (5:4-5)?

_____

_____

_____

_____

_____

The world can be a difficult place. Pressure from friends and relatives, our sinful nature, frustrating circumstances, financial strain, and countless other irritations and temptations drag us down daily. Those who don't know Christ face a difficult (and for many, a meaningless) struggle against their problems. The good news is that with God's help, we can defeat the world. We don't have to lose, give in, or give up. We can be victorious. Because we belong to Christ, we can overcome all of life's obstacles. This is what makes being a Christian worthwhile.

REALIZE
the principle

5 In 5:4-5, what is meant by "the world"?

_____

_____

_____

_____

_____

6 What does it mean for a Christian to "defeat" the world?

_____

_____

_____

_____

_____

7 Many Christians think obeying God is difficult. Why is that a misconception (5:3)?

_____

_____

_____

_____

8 Why do we sometimes think obeying God is difficult?

_____

_____

_____

_____

9 How does faith (trusting God) make life easier?

_____

_____

_____

_____

RESPOND
to the message

10 What people or circumstances have kept you from feeling as if you have defeated the world?

_____

_____

_____

_____

_____

11 What difficulties in life does faith in Christ enable you to overcome?

_____

_____

_____

_____

_____

12 In what battles do you want to be victorious?

_____

_____

_____

_____

_____

13 What can you do to strengthen your faith?

_____

_____

_____

_____

_____

A What does it mean that Jesus Christ "was revealed as God's Son by his baptism in water and by shedding his blood" (5:6)? Why is this important to your Christian faith?

B How can we have eternal life (5:11-12)? What does the promise of eternal life mean to you?

LESSON 11
PRAYING FOR OTHERS
1 JOHN 5:13-21

REFLECT
on your life

1 How did you learn to pray?

_____

_____

_____

_____

_____

2 Who taught you?

_____

_____

_____

_____

READ
the passage

Read 1 John 5:13-21 and the following notes:

❐ 5:14, 15   ❐ 5:16, 17   ❐ 5:18, 19

3 Why can we as Christians have confidence when we pray (5:14)?

_____

_____

_____

_____

4 Why is it important to pray for our brothers and sisters in Christ (5:16-17)?

_____

_____

_____

_____

_____

John concluded his letter with a clear statement about prayer (5:13-15). God wants to work through us, and one of the ways he does this is through our prayers. Of course, the purpose of prayer is to shape our will to his, not his will to ours. As we pray for his will to be done, he listens and responds to our requests. And we have the assurance that when we ask for his will, particularly in the lives of other Christians, he will grant what we ask. Our Christian brothers and sisters need us to intercede for them. Every need in a fellow Christian's life is an occasion to pray.

REALIZE
the principle

5 How is praying for others an important part of loving them?

_____

_____

_____

_____

6 What might cause us to feel discouraged when we pray for others?

_____

_____

_____

_____

_____

7 What truths about God encourage us to pray?

_____

_____

_____

_____

_____

RESPOND
to the message

8 When is it easy to pray for others?

_____

_____

_____

9 When is it difficult to pray for others?

_____

_____

_____

_____

10 How can we be sure to ask for "anything that pleases him [God]" (5:14) when we pray for others?

_____

_____

_____

_____

11 When you tell someone, "I'll pray for you," what practical steps can you take to make sure you will actually do it?

_____

_____

_____

_____

_____

RESOLVE
to take action

12 List those whom you can pray for this week. What are their needs?

_____

_____

_____

_____

_____

A How can you know you have eternal life (5:13)? Whom do you know who needs this assurance? How could you share Christ with that person?

B What is the sin that leads to death (5:16-17)? How can this help you pray for others?

C What has impressed you about the book of 1 John? How has it most affected your habits and lifestyle?

MORE
for studying
other themes
in this section

LESSON 12
WATCH OUT!
2 JOHN

REFLECT
on your life

1 What are some of the warning signs around your house (e.g., on appliances, power tools, household cleaning products)?

_____

_____

_____

_____

_____

_____

2 What is something you wish you had been warned against?

_____

_____

_____

_____

_____

READ
the passage

Read the introduction to 2 John, the book of 2 John, and the following notes:

❐ 1:3, 4   ❐ 1:7   ❐ 1:8   ❐ 1:10

3 Study the Megathemes "Truth" and "Love." In your own words, describe the importance of truth and love to Christians.

Truth _____

_____

_____

_____

Love _____

_____

_____

_____

4 What were the "deceivers" teaching (1:7)?

_____

_____

_____

_____

_____

5 How are believers to treat false teachers (1:10, 11)?

_____

_____

_____

_____

_____

_____

The traveling preachers of John's day relied on the hospitality of Christians for food and shelter. But John warned his readers not to open their homes to just any person claiming to be a Christian teacher. In fact, false teachers deserved no acceptance or hospitality at all. While we demonstrate our love for God by loving one another, we also demonstrate it by rejecting teachers who misrepresent him and lead people astray. Accepting and welcoming false teachers only legitimizes their false teaching. Out of love for God and others who may be influenced by false teachers, we must be careful not to support those who teach wrong ideas about God and the Christian life.

REALIZE
the principle

6 Why are false teachers so dangerous?

_____

_____

_____

_____

_____

7 What dangers are there in believing what is not true?

_____

_____

_____

_____

8 What happens when Christians follow false teachers?

_____

_____

_____

_____

R
RESPOND
to the message

9 How do Christians support false teachers?

_____

_____

_____

_____

_____

10 Why are people often tempted to take false teaching lightly?

_____

_____

_____

_____

_____

11 What would you do if a close friend became a member of a cult or began to follow a false teacher?

_____

_____

_____

_____

12 How can we screen organizations before donating money to them?

_____

_____

_____

_____

13 What ministry or minister does 2 John challenge you to screen, reexamine, or support more fully?

RESOLVE
to take action

_____

_____

_____

_____

A John placed a strong emphasis on truth in this letter. What advantages are there to living according to an absolute standard of truth?

MORE
for studying
other themes
in this section

B How can Christians be loving and kind while refusing to accept false teachers? How might this affect the way you interact with your religious non-Christian friends?

LESSON 13
OPEN HOMES
3 JOHN

REFLECT
on your life

1 What makes you feel welcome and comfortable in someone's home?

_____

_____

_____

_____

_____

_____

READ
the passage

Read the introduction to 3 John, the book of 3 John, and the following notes:

❑ 1:1 ❑ 1:5, 6 ❑ 1:7 ❑ 1:8 ❑ 1:9, 10 ❑ 1:12 ❑ 1:14

2 Describe each of the people mentioned in this letter:

Gaius (1:1-8) _____

_____

_____

Diotrephes (1:9-10) _____

_____

_____

Demetrius (1:12) _____

_____

_____

3 In John's day, how did Christians show hospitality to traveling teachers?

_____

_____

_____

_____

In the days of the early church, those who made a living meeting the spiritual needs of God's people depended on their generosity. How did Christians give support? Hospitality—housing and feeding the traveling teachers during their stay. In many ways, hospitality has become a lost art in our day. Some people may be afraid of having their house messed up, some don't want the inconvenience, and some may just not want to take the time. For whatever reason, many people have closed their homes to visitors. But part of showing Christ's love to others is to be hospitable—to share what we have with those in need.

REALIZE
the principle

4 Many people feel uneasy about offering hospitality. What reasons have you heard people give for not opening up their homes to others?

_____

_____

_____

_____

_____

5 What does having an open home achieve?

_____

_____

_____

_____

_____

6 What barriers hold you back from being hospitable?

_____

_____

_____

_____

RESPOND
to the message

7 What are some creative ways you can show hospitality?

_____

_____

_____

_____

_____

_____

8 Who could benefit from your hospitality?

_____

_____

_____

_____

_____

_____

RESOLVE
to take action

9 John wrote, "Dear friend, you are being faithful to God when you care for the traveling teachers" (1:5). What act of hospitality could you perform this week?

_____

_____

_____

_____

_____

_____

MORE
for studying
other themes
in this section

A How was Diotrephes a danger to the church (1:9-10)? What examples of this have you seen in the church today? What steps should be taken against people like Diotrephes?

B Why were Gaius and Demetrius commended by John (1:1-8, 12)? Whom would you commend for similar reasons?